CELEBRATING THE PSALMS

RICHARD GORDON

Published by New Generation Publishing in 2018

Copyright © Richard Gordon 2018

First Edition

Front cover photographic art by Jonny Magowan copyright JonnyM
Productions 2018

www.newgeneration-publishing.com

 New Generation Publishing

Celebrating the Psalms is dedicated to two very inspirational women, Moreen Gordon and Ruth Magowan.

PREFACE

This book has arisen out of a lifetime spent teaching the Old Testament and ministering to students and to established congregations in Kenya, Malawi and Ireland. Celebrating the Psalms is both an academic work and a devotional one. It has been written for theological students, for working ministers and for those leading Bible studies on the Psalms.

Rev Dr Richard N. Gordon

Bachelor of Science (Queen's University, Belfast) 1958; Diploma in Education (Queen's University, Belfast) 1963; Bachelor of Divinity, (London University External), 1966; Doctor of Philosophy in Biblical Studies (Queen's University, Belfast) 1975.

Along with 80 years spent at the University of Life!

ACKNOWLEDGEMENTS

This book has two parents – the first is a text book on Psalms which arose from teaching the Old Testament at Zomba Theological College in Malawi from 1995 to 2000 which was entitled *Transforming Psalms*, and the second was *Psalms for Sadness, Sickness and Celebration* which was a more devotional approach highlighting 20 of the shorter psalms with each accompanied by a beautiful photograph and a short prayer.

I am indebted to the staff and students of Zomba Theological College and the Kachere Press in Zomba for making the first book possible. The second was the brainchild of Pearl Hutchinson who also took the photographs. Creating and writing that book was a great privilege.

Without the help of many people this third book, *Celebrating the Psalms*, would never have seen the light of day! I gratefully acknowledge the help of my editor, Ruth Magowan, along with the detailed proof reading and suggested corrections and improvements by Dr Brian Magowan.

I also gladly acknowledge the huge encouragement from numerous family members, particularly those of Clare Gordon and Professor Melita Gordon as well as Jonny Magowan and John Seddon.

I am greatly indebted to the Reverend Rosemary Frew who read right through an initial manuscript and made a number of most valuable suggestions, almost all of which have been incorporated in the final draft.

It is acknowledged that no book of this kind is the work of one person but rather the author is dependent upon and indebted to many who have gone before. I have sought to acknowledge my indebtedness for all direct quotations and have included specific references wherever possible. I apologise for any omissions. To all of you, thank you!

CONTENTS

INTRODUCTION

There is no book in the Bible which more accurately reflects the varieties of human behaviour than the Psalms. Those who wrote them had experienced life in its fullness. There are angry psalms and contented psalms; there are psalms about success and psalms about failure; there are psalms about riches and poverty, about greed and generosity, about coping and not coping; there are psalms about sickness and health; there are many sad psalms and there are many psalms of praise and thanksgiving.

Within the Psalter there is temper and patience, there is frustration and acceptance, there is revolt and submission, and there is holiness and rebellion. The psalmists are teachers in the school of unselfish living – and the lessons they deliver are very important lessons and ones that only those who live close to God are able to learn. The psalmists have been there, and know trials and temptations, moods and tensions and all the hang-ups that can occur in human living. Articulated in the psalms are the solace for wounds, recipes for forgiveness of sins, and foundations for joy and thanksgiving - in fact appropriate words, thoughts, prayers, along with appropriate tears and laughter, for every human situation and condition.

For three thousand years these psalms have taught the community of faith how to express their religious and irreligious feelings to God and have thereby enabled believers, both Jew and Christian, to come to terms with the worst and the best that life has offered to them, bringing it all before the One they dare to call 'Our dear heavenly Father'. Indeed, the psalmists teach how to pray to 'Our dear Heavenly Father' who is a righteous and merciful God. Like all Israel's moral teachers, they declare to their readers that God blesses righteous obedient people and that sin and disobedience deserve punishment. Psalm 18 is a classic statement of this commandment to live righteously, verses 20-21 are typical:

> The Lord rewarded me according to my righteousness;
> According to the cleanness of my hands he recompensed me.
> For I have kept the ways of the Lord,
> And have not wickedly departed from my God.

Christians read psalms looking for, and finding, words that are

1

fulfilled in Christ. They find them a comfort and strength and a guiding hand when they are uncertain or distressed. They were written to provide proper vehicles for needy worshippers in every possible human circumstance, and Christian worshippers have taken these pre-Christian songs and brought to them the rich promises of Christ. Psalms have always enjoyed a prominent place in the Church's praise, but they arguably deserve a greater place in the teaching, preaching and thinking of Christian leaders, and will always enrich their songs of praise. It is good to read from the Psalms every day and allow them to gradually inform the mind, the heart and the soul.

Not only the community of faith, however, but many others have found solace and challenge, light and truth, and the exuberance of the human spirit set forth in the Psalter. How marvellous it would be to know all the psalms off by heart! But if that is beyond most people, everyone can at least appreciate, enjoy and be enriched by reading them with more understanding and devotion.

CHAPTER ONE

WHAT ARE THE PSALMS?

The Psalms are a collection of ancient hymns and holy songs originally written in Hebrew by the people of Israel over the centuries between 1100 BC until 300 BC. The collection was, and still is, the Hymn Book of the Jewish People in the form of the first book of the Writings, the third section of the Hebrew Bible. It is also an important book in the Christian Old Testament.

The people of Israel were initially a wandering people, then slaves in Egypt, then a conquering nation, a divided people, a deported population, a returning remnant and finally an optimistic band of pilgrims. These hymns or holy songs were sung to tunes long since forgotten, and nowhere recorded, by the Jews in Old Testament Times (OTT)[1] in their Temple in Jerusalem and in their synagogues throughout the Ancient Near East. Subsequently they have also been sung by Christians since the time of the disciples in the first century A.D.

The Psalter is the collective name given to the Book of Psalms. Like many hymns books the Psalter contains a wide variety of sacred songs, which were written over a long period of time, by a variety of people, and to meet many different needs. They are now sung, recited, and read in a variety of different ways - from plain-song to folk tunes, to recitation, and even to pop tunes. The group which probably makes most extensive use of the psalms is the Benedictine Order whose members sing and recite all of every psalm every week, following the example and instruction of their founder, St. Benedict of Nursia in the 6th century A.D.

The variety of psalms is wide. Many were written for formal liturgical use in the Temple; others will have been adopted from earlier originals and subsequently used in worship, while still others will have been used in teaching the Jewish faith and way of life to the young and

---

[1]'OT' denotes the 39 books of the Old Testament whereas 'OTT' (Old Testament Times) is an abbreviation defining both the places where the psalms originated, and the centuries during which they were written.

to interested enquirers. Included are prayers, praises, history and prophecy, as well as proverbial wisdom and love songs.

The excitement of these holy songs is that they have met human need for millennia, and they still meet human need today. At a first reading these poems may seem alien to 21st century ears yet, wonderfully, as the reader gains confidence and familiarity with them, they become increasingly relevant, powerful and beautiful.

There are about 150 songs (the need to be approximate will emerge later!) and, in the Bible, they form the largest book. They vary greatly in length and in style. This becomes apparent from even an initial reading. They are grouped into five collections which are presumed to have been made separately at different times and places by at least five different people. Each collection has distinctive characteristics. In the Psalter, they are called Books I, II, III, IV and V and are numbered:

- Book I from Ps 1 to Ps 41
- Book II from Ps 42 to Ps 72
- Book III from Ps 73 to Ps 89
- Book IV from Ps 90 to Ps 106
- And Book V from Ps 107 to Ps 150

Part of the fascination of psalm study has been to speculate about the original usage and purpose of each holy song. Many of them are thought to have been composed for particular Jewish religious occasions in the Jerusalem Temple. The Jews' great annual festivals were marked with special Temple services. The main festivals were the Passover with its accompanying Day of Atonement, the Feast of Unleavened bread, the Feast of Tabernacles, and the Feast of Weeks or Pentecost. To these might be added an Annual Enthronement occasion when God's rule over Israel was thought to have been celebrated and when the earthly king's position as God's regent was also recognised. A majority of the psalms were probably first used at one or other of these occasions.

The psalms were originally written in classical Hebrew, were then translated into Aramaic and Greek, and subsequently into all the languages in which the Bible is now read. They are scripture, prayer and praise and although the majority of them are found in the Book of Psalms there are also a few additional psalms to be found in other Old and New Testament Books. All of these are only a small part of the total number that will have been written by Jews and Christians over their

4

long histories. The Book of Psalms has had a great influence on the New Testament and many psalms are quoted in the New Testament. In a very real sense Psalms forms a bridge between the Old and the New Testaments. This is substantiated by the knowledge of them demonstrated by Jesus and his first disciples and all who wrote New Testament books.

In order to navigate around the Psalter there are general questions which can be usefully asked, and the answers to these questions will emerge in the subsequent pages of this book. Who were the psalms written for? What exactly where they written for? What different types of psalms are there? And how did they come to be arranged in five different 'books' each with its particular distinguishing characteristics?

Additional questions will be asked of each individual psalm and answers will be suggested in Chapter 8. When was the psalm written, who wrote it, what was it written for, what type was it, was it a prayer or a meditation or even a lesson, and was it for individuals or for congregational use? Perhaps most interestingly of all, what was the original and what the contemporary applications of each psalm?

These songs are a commentary on life over the period they were written. They contain a range of some of the responses that believers made to God over that long period. In some ways, they are a parallel to that more formal history recorded in the historical books of the Old Testament (Genesis to 2nd Chronicles). They have been found to be appropriate praise in every generation since.

Psalm Functions

The psalms have had particular functions for believers ever since they were written. The majority were intended for use in worship. They are the responses of believing people to their God. This God of whom the psalmists speak is the One who created the world out of nothing, who delivered his chosen people out of slavery in Egypt, who led this people to their promised land and who through the Law and the Prophets progressively revealed himself to them. Some of these songs recite Israel's history of which Jews are intensely proud; others are more like sacred anthems with opportunity for responses by the worshippers. Some psalms are songs of repentance. Many of them are the prayers and the cries and the praises of the children of Israel to their God whom they called *Yahweh*. Some will have been used by a congregation and others by individuals. Psalm 120.1,2 for instance is an example of an individual psalm:

> In my distress I cry to the Lord, that he may answer me;
> Deliver me, O Lord, from lying lips, and a deceitful tongue.

Ps 22.1 is a very well-known example of a highly individualistic prayer subsequently uttered by Jesus of Nazareth on the Cross at Calvary:

> My God, my God, why hast thou forsaken me?
> Why art thou so far from helping me from the words of my groaning?

These highly charged words express for all time the degree of alienation that Jesus Christ was prepared to suffer on behalf of mankind in order the redeem the world.

Psalm language and vocabulary

The Psalter is an integral part of the Holy Bible. That context allows the reader to make a beginning in understanding the psalms. The language comes from Old Testament Times – this useful phrase identifies the time, the place and the circumstances which produced the psalms. The time is from the 12th C BC to the 4th C BC, the place is the Middle East, and the context is the Bible. The original language was classical Hebrew which eventually died out but a modern form of this ancient language was re-introduced in the 20th C AD by the Israeli Government in an attempt to unify the very diverse group of Jews now living in Palestine, a people who have come from all over the world.

Even in translation we may come across words with which we are not familiar. Often the way things are expressed in the Bible and the very words used are not those used in every day speech and writing. When psalms are read they are Scripture, it is a religious language which arose out of a particular historical situation.

Hebrew poetry

In common with poetry in many languages, Hebrew poets feel freer to use language metaphorically, allegorically, and symbolically than do those authors who confine themselves to writing in prose. The Old Testament prophet Isaiah, as well as the psalmists, makes powerful use of allegory in his poetic prophecies. In Isaiah 5.1-7 he uses the allegory of the vine that Jesus was to use centuries later to describe the people of God. Ps 1.3 is an example of allegory used in the psalms:

He is like a tree, planted by streams of water,
That yields its fruit in its season, and its leaf does not wither.

One of the particular devices used by Hebrew poets is called **parallelism**. This simply means that ideas are repeated, developed or even contradicted in successive lines in order to reinforce the meaning. Almost every psalm uses parallelism e.g. from Ps 91.2

The Lord reigns, he is robed in majesty,
The Lord is robed, he is girded with strength.

Here there are two inter-relating pairs of parallels. The whole effect is poetic, and the metaphor of a robed God is powerful to any people accustomed to a robed monarch being splendidly adorned and certainly Solomon and his successors would have been. Ps 93.3 is an example of triple parallelism which is stair-like.

The floods have lifted up O Lord
The floods have lifted up their voice
The floods lift up their roaring.

Rhyme, rhythm and regular verse length are some of the characteristic of traditional English poetry. In Hebrew poetry parallelism and other devices are used in the original Hebrew of the psalms and although rhythm may be detected, its impact will be reduced in translation. The occurrence of rhyme where the final **syllables of a line** sound similar is absent in Hebrew poetry although use is made of similar sounding words. Whereas verses are very often the same length in English poetry, this is not so in Hebrew poetry.

In any language, poetry has great potential to open up new dimensions of meaning and of beauty. Poetry offers the reader language and images that help to make the message clear and stimulate the imagination and the soul. Poetry both delights and instructs. The poetry of the psalms tells stories and paints pictures. Perhaps many people can understand meaning more easily than they can appreciate beauty. The psalms have both meaning and beauty. But poetry makes more demands

7

upon the reader than ordinary prose and this may account for the fact that many people come to the psalms later in life. Eugene Peterson (1987) commented that poetry is 'language used with intensity which drags us into the depths of reality'! (Pg11-12)

Psalm titles, authorship and dates

In many modern versions of the Bible there are titles appearing at the beginning of the majority of the psalms. (usually in slightly smaller type). The 34 without titles are termed 'orphan psalms'! The titles are not as old as the psalms themselves but are included in the Masoretic Text from which all subsequent translations were made. This Masoretic text can be dated to the 9thC AD. In New Testament times Temple worship was still flourishing and there are many references in the New Testament to King David having written particular psalms. The titles, and in particular the Davidic authorship, of Psalms have been keenly debated for many years.

The 116 psalms which do have titles vary in length and in content. They include notes about the assumed author, instructions about musical accompaniment and about the type of the psalm. One group of scholars gives them almost complete credibility and authority on a par with the psalm text that follows. They imply that they are very little younger and of almost equal importance. At the other extreme the editors and translators of the New English Bible (published in 1970) leave them out. Most experts adopt an intermediate position and one such would be the New Century Bible Commentary on Psalms by A.A. Anderson (1972) who says that, although the titles (sometimes called superscriptions) were certainly in place by the 9th C AD when the Hebrew text was edited by the Masoretes and the vocalisation was added, it is not known at what intermediate date these superscriptions were actually appended. Opinion is divided. These titles attach David's name to 73 psalms and also mention other authors including the sons of Korah, Asaph, Solomon and even Moses (Ps 90). There is no claim anywhere in the Bible that King David wrote all the psalms although there is the tradition that calls the whole biblical book the Psalms of David. The evidence that the 73 that are ascribed to David, were at least connected with him has the following supporting evidence:

In 1 Samuel 16.14ff it is recorded that David came to King Saul's attention due to the fact that he was a skilled musician

In the New Testament Jesus and various New Testament authors, including St Paul, attribute at least some psalms to David

All 73 superscriptions include the phrase 'of David'

However, it has been pointed out by many Hebrew language scholars that 'of David' is ambiguous and can mean at least the following;

Written by David, or
Written for David, or
Collected by David, or
Collected in honour of David, or
Attributed to one of David's successors i.e. someone of the Davidic line of kings.

Over the past 250 years majority opinion has changed and currently more scholars now accept the early date of many of the 73 psalms attributed to David and therefore the possibility that he wrote at least some of them. Absolute proof is not available and undoubtedly different opinions will continue to be held. These psalms will all be ascribed to the early pre-exilic period. Very often the identity of the psalmist is not known and all that can be said that the unknown psalmist will have been a priest or Levitical singer in the Temple, or a prophet linked to the Temple or sometimes that he belonged to a group known as the 'Wise men'.

If the date on which a psalm had been written could be determined then this would give a great deal of help in determining the authorship. However precise dating will probably never be possible and currently most scholars date psalms approximately as 'early or late pre-exilic,' 'exilic,' or 'early or late post-exilic'. The Exile referred to was the deportation and captivity of many of the people of Judah by the Babylonians from 586 - 537 BC.

The Psalms and the Jerusalem Temple

The Psalter has frequently been called the Hymn Book of the Second Temple. The first Temple was built by King Solomon in about 950 BC. This was destroyed by the Babylonians in 586 BC and on the return from exile in about 540 BC the Second Temple was built slowly and completed by about 516 BC (it is sometimes called Zerubbabel's Temple after the Babylonian Governor at the time, who made a large donation towards the re-building). It was during the period of the

9

Second Temple that the psalms were collected and extensively used in Temple worship day by day. The affection of the Jews for their Temple was powerfully expressed in many psalms, Ps 84.1,2 is a good example:

How lovely is thy dwelling place, O Lord of hosts?
My soul longs, yea faints, for the courts of the Lord
My heart and flesh sing for joy to the living God,

and so too is Ps 84.10

For a day in thy courts is better than a thousand elsewhere.
I would rather be a door keeper in the house of my God
Than dwell in the tents of wickedness.

The Second Temple was destroyed by the Romans in about 70 AD and has never been rebuilt. After the Exile although the Temple was still the primary focus of Jewish worship, synagogue worship became more significant and the psalms would also have been sung and recited in synagogues throughout the land and wherever there was a congregation of worshipping Jews. The Temple had been that for which they had yearned during the long dreary years in captivity in Babylon. It was also the Temple where the praises of Israel reached their climax. Ps 150 is the doxology for the whole Psalter and is, as it were, almost a recording of a Temple praise concert:

Praise the Lord!
Praise God in his sanctuary
Praise him in his mighty firmament
Praise him for his mighty deeds
Praise him according to his exceeding greatness.

Precise information about the relation of the Psalms to the Temple is lacking but certainly psalms played a significant role in early Jerusalem worship in the Temple e.g. Hannah's Prayer 1 Samuel 2.1-10. It is also known that David commissioned Levitical singers including Asaph, and 12 psalms are attributed to Asaph in the psalm titles i.e. Psalms 50, and 73-83. In summary quoting Oxford Biblical Studies, "The Temple and the Psalms are inextricably tied to one another."

Psalm scholarship from the 19th Century

No book about psalms would be complete without recording the debt due to the great German Psalm scholar Hermann Gunkel (1862-1932) and his Norwegian pupil Sigmund Mowinckel (1884 – 1965). Both, with differing emphases, brought Psalm study back into the centre of Old Testament study. Prior to their work the psalms had been increasingly downgraded as late compositions. These two established that the psalms were indeed written over a long period of time and that many were pre-exilic compositions.

Divisions and Collections within the Psalter

In the Bible, the Psalter is divided into five collections or books, as mentioned previously. These divisions are older than the titles which have been added later and some believe the divisions are analogous to the first five books of the Bible, the five Books of Moses i.e. Genesis, Exodus, Leviticus, Numbers and Deuteronomy. Some distinctive characteristics of these five groups will now be noted and some other groupings of psalms will also be identified. Each 'book' ends with a doxology. Ps 1 and probably Ps 2 are introductions to the whole Psalter, and Ps 150 and perhaps Ps 149 a conclusion to the whole.

Book I Mainly pre-exilic, with almost all the psalms attributed to King David and YAHWEH as the predominate god-name, translated as the LORD (in capital letters) in many contemporary translations.

Book II Mainly pre-exilic, with ELOHIM the predominate god-name, translated 'God' in most versions

Book III Mainly exilic with Ps 137 as the classic example of an exilic psalm

Book IV Mainly pre-exilic

Book V Mainly post-exilic

It is understood that the five Books were originally separate collections probably made by different people, at different times in different places. All five were brought together at some time shortly after the Second Temple was completed.

In addition to the five 'books' there are other collections within the Psalter crossing over the 'books' divisions

Davidic collection	Ps 3-41; Ps 51-72; Ps 138-145 all attributed to David as previously discussed
Korahite collection	Ps 42-49; 84-85; 87-88 attributed to Korah - there are four 'Korahs' in the Old Testament. The one mentioned in the superscriptions is thought to be the grandson of Levi, and many Korahites held responsible posts in the Temple particularly associated with Temple music.
Elohistic collection	Ps 42-83 (see above)
Asaphite collection	Ps 73-83
Psalms on the kingship of God	Ps 93-100
A collection of psalms of praise	Ps 103-107
Songs of Ascent	Ps 120-134
Hallelujah psalms	Ps 111-118; 146-150
The Great Hallel	Ps 113-118

Psalms and their music

It is no longer possible to reproduce the music of the Second Temple. Therefore, although many of the psalms have musical directions in the appended headings, it is not known what the music was, although some of the instruments used are known (see e.g. Ps 150).

Conclusion

The psalms are all, in one way or another, responses by worshipping individuals and a worshipping community to the initiatives of God in every age, including our own. Bernard Anderson (1983) quotes the words of Augustine from the 4th C AD "Thou movest us to delight in praising thee, for thou hast formed us for thyself, and our hearts are restless until they find their rest in thee." So, whether we think of the deep penitence of Ps 51:

> Have mercy on me O God, according to thy steadfast love;
> According to thy abundant mercy blot out my transgressions

or, the exuberant joy of worship in Ps 84, in the metrical version,

> How lovely is thy dwelling place O Lord of hosts to me.

here are faithful souls responding to a loving heavenly Father. And although Ps 45 is an exception to many of the other psalms in that it is thought to have been written to celebrate a royal wedding and probably sung in a palace rather than a temple, it is nevertheless a moving response to what God has done:

> My heart overflows with a goodly theme,
> I address my verses to the king
> My tongue is like the pen of a ready scribe

This song was ascribed to a king but it is also a response to a loving heavenly Father, who allowed such a king to rule.

DISCUSSION TOPIC

Find out more about the relationship of King David to the Book of Psalms.

CHAPTER TWO

HOW TO READ THE PSALMS

These pages are written to allow readers to discover for themselves some of the incomparable riches offered in the psalms and with the hope that they will develop a deeper appreciation of Israel's holy songs. As their love for the psalms grows they will discover that the book has the capacity to change them - their thoughts, their prayers, their words and even their deeds. It is only as knowledge of the Book of Psalms grows that the psalms will be able to weave their work of change.

There are people, some of whom are within the Church, and others who are too honest to claim that privilege, who find the psalms, and probably most of the Bible too difficult, too boring and too irrelevant to try and understand. Yes, they may have dipped into the Scriptures briefly at some time, but lost heart, for there was no immediate dividend. Or perhaps they were thrust into the Scriptures by well-meaning relatives or friends and got lost. This book invites them to try again to ask some questions and, with prayer, hope for some answers.

There is a proverb which says, "Learning comes through work."[2] In order to become familiar with the psalms and allow them to *transform* their lives, readers will want to use them every day. Only by using them will they remember them and only by remembering them will they learn how to apply them. In order to use the psalms and to enjoy them to best effect in their lives, they will have to be prepared to work at acquiring a deeper knowledge of them. The Bible reading habit and learning about the psalms calls for perseverance. Most people will be able to read one psalm each day except for the longer ones.[3]

Poetry makes more demands upon the reader than prose, and the psalms are poetry and songs which have been translated from another language, have been written at another time, in another place and from another religion, and may therefore require a more sustained effort by the reader.[4] Getting to know the psalms is both slow and rewarding.

---

[2] Ancient Irish proverb
[3] The six longest are 119, 78, 89, 18, 105, and 106.
[4] H. Cunliffe Jones, *Torch Commentaries - Jeremiah*, London: SCM, 1960, p.16 comments on the study of biblical poetry generally that, "the sustained

Take heart, there are very few people who would consider themselves experts!

The reader will want to try to enter this new world, which is the world of the Patriarchs and Moses, the Exodus, the Kings and the Prophets. It is the world of the Exile and the Return and the reader will want to understand a world where Israel, a holy nation, entered the 'Holy Land' and eliminated the peoples who had previously lived there; and that this has been resented by the displaced nations ever since, and that the origins of our contemporary political conflicts in the Middle East go back at least 3500 years.

For Christians, the most dramatic change in the use of the psalms will have been when the early Christians adopted the whole Psalter for use as its first hymn book, and understood the psalms in the light of the Messiah having come in the person of Jesus Christ. For this reason, the Psalter remains one of the most effective bridges between the Old Testament and the New Testament.

1. Traditional and contemporary uses

Prayer, praise and scripture reading have always been the three of the principle ways of using the psalms in both the private and public worship of God.

The majority of the psalms are prayers.[5] Ps 103 is an example. The final three verses make a fitting end to many prayers:

> Bless the Lord, O you his angels,
> You mighty ones who do his word,
> Hearkening to the voice of his word!
> Bless the Lord, all his hosts,
> His ministers that do His will!
> Bless the Lord, all his works,
> In all places of his dominion.
> Bless the Lord, O my soul! Amen.

There are many moments in each of our lives when the words of this

---

attention that must be given to poetry, though once they are familiar the poetry lays hold upon the mind with a greater power than prose".

[5] Approximately 90-100 are prayers, depending on whether the whole psalm is a prayer or simply a part is a prayer.

psalm can be used, and it is no accident that these words are used often in public prayer. Prayer life will be very much richer when passages from the psalms can be recalled for use when a seeker wants to talk to God. For those who are called on to pray in public, psalm language brings an added richness, piety and depth to prayers, and avoids the dangers of repetition and monotony.

The psalms have been used as praise throughout all the Jewish and Christian centuries. When congregations assemble they sing psalms, and choirs have sung them in plain song or in parts in every century. Individual believers who are musical, and those who are not, also sing the psalms as they walk through life. Psalm 95 is an explicit example:

O come, let us sing to the Lord;
Let us make a joyful noise to the rock of our salvation!
Let us come into his presence with thanksgiving;
Let us make a joyful noise to him with songs of praise!

The psalms can be sung in church in many ways. They can be sung both unaccompanied and also in the more biblical way of accompanied singing. Ps 150 is the authority and the precedent for accompanied singing.

Praise him with trumpet sound;
Praise him with lute and harp!
Praise him with timbrel and dance;
Praise him with strings and pipe!
Praise him with sounding cymbals;
Praise him with loud clashing cymbals!

Since the Reformation in the 16th C. AD the psalms have been sung in their metrical version especially by Presbyterian churches throughout the world. Classically they have been sung unaccompanied often employing folk tunes.

The original instruments used included harp, trumpet, flute, pipe, horn, lyre.[6] The psalms were read in the Temple and in synagogues and in churches as part of every liturgy and service. The Word of God, read and heard, is in itself a proclamation of the Gospel and can be a profession of faith by those who read or listen. Reading has many

---

[6] see Psalm 150

possible variations. It may be done by an individual, or by a congregation in unison; it may be done responsively, and in some of the Episcopal denominations the psalms, like the Gospel, are intoned in plain song. The study, the teaching, and the preaching of the psalms arise out of the psalms being heard. These exercises can be devotional, intellectual and academic.

Not all of the psalms are applicable to every situation and the classification of psalms into those which are primarily individual and those which are communal is a useful division when finding psalms which are appropriate. Ps 120 is a highly individualistic little psalm and it is difficult to imagine its use in public worship.

> In my distress, I cry to the Lord,
> that he may answer me:
> "Deliver me, O Lord,
> from lying lips,
> from a deceitful tongue."
> What shall be given to you?
> And what more shall be done to you,
> You deceitful tongue?
> A warrior's sharp arrows,
> with glowing coals of the broom tree! (Ps. 120.1-4)

However, it is not only the psalms that are written in the plural which are communal psalms. Many of the psalms written in the singular are clearly appropriate for congregational use. The best-known example is Psalm 23 which is written in the singular but countless generations of congregations have witnessed to their spiritual gain as they have sung it together.

> The Lord is my shepherd, I shall not want;
> He makes me to lie down in green pastures.
> He leads me beside the still waters;
> He restores my soul. (Ps 23.1-2)

It is as the psalms are known better that you, the reader, becomes more aware of what is appropriate in any given situation. The Bibles published by the Gideon Association have very clear guidelines on the uses of Scripture including, of course, the psalms.

2. Psalm order

A convincing explanation of the order in which the psalms occur in the Bible has frustrated orderly minds for many years, for initially there appears to be little order at all. It is true that in the first two Books there are more psalms of an early date with a connection to David, of a Lament type, and which use the oldest word for God (Yahweh). There are more, longer, praising, and perhaps later dated psalms further on in the Book but, having said that, these divisions are far from absolute. It is also true that more psalms bearing titles are included in Books I - III and more of the so called 'orphan' psalms, which bear no titles, are to be found in Books IV - V. It is better to come to the study of psalms admitting that we are far from clear about many things. The study of psalm arrangement has a long history and there were clearly other earlier, shorter and perhaps geographically based collections from which finally our Psalter emerged in all its wonder and with all its riches.

3. Words for God used in the Psalter

At least four different words are used for God in the psalms. They are 'el', 'Elohim', 'Adonai', and 'Yahweh'. They are translated as God or god, lord and LORD. Much has been written about the particular significance of these four. Probably Yahweh (in the Hebrew spelt with no vowels to emphasize the reluctance of the Israelites to 'name' God) is the most reverential of the four terms and it is usually translated in most English versions as LORD (except the Jerusalem Bible which writes 'Yahweh'). Elohim is used in many places, and used with much greater frequency in the Elohistic collection Ps 42 – 83, and is translated as God. Yahweh is used more often in Book I. So, Yahweh is the preferred God-name in Book I and Elohim preferred for Book II and part of Book III. Adonai is usually rendered as Lord, and el or Elohim will be used to designate the gods of other nations. Sometimes the expression Yahweh Elohim is used (as in Ps 59.5 where it is translated in English as LORD, God of hosts.) Yahweh is used very often on its own e.g. Ps 107.13 and many other places. Elohim on its own also occurs frequently e.g. Ps 139.19.

4. Psalm Categories

The study of psalm **types** has been explored intensively for about 150 years; this still continues and the results are far from conclusive. The French word *genre* or family is normally used to identify all those texts we call psalms. The English word, *type* and the German word *gattungen* are usually reserved to describe the different kinds of psalm within the genre of psalm. The **classification** of psalms has intrigued psalm scholars and often perplexed readers for a long time and, up to this point in time, no one has as yet produced a foolproof or perfect classification that was definitive and fully acceptable. The contemporary view prefers division into a small number of types of psalm. One modern study simply divides them into psalms of praise and psalms of lament with the addition of some subsidiary groups. More of this later - but sufficient to say at this stage that, when we attempt to put the psalms into categories, we find that many defy easy cataloguing as they can be variously classified i.e. many psalms sound several notes simultaneously and are therefore recognisable as **Mixed** types. In this book, we shall follow an arrangement which recognises the following main types of psalms.

4.1 Laments and related types

There are about sixty psalms in this type. Included are the six or seven psalms designated by Christians as Penitential Psalms (Ps. 6, 32, 38, 51, 102, 130 and 143) and twenty or so 'Cursing' psalms of which two of the most notorious are 69.22-33, and 137.9. These psalms are all aware of the plight, danger or tragedy of individuals or groups. The words 'moan' or 'complaint' have also been used to describe the group. These psalms cry out to the living God, and plead that God will listen to his suffering children. These are the psalms to turn to in sadness, sickness and worry. The large number of these psalms is a reflection of the hardness of life for many people. There are countless occasions when the psalmists' words provide exactly what is needed as either individuals or as congregations, when there is a need to open hearts in agony before God. How often the cry is needed:

> O Lord, rebuke me not in thy anger, nor chasten me in thy wrath.
> Be gracious to me, O Lord, for I am languishing;
> O Lord, heal me, for my bones are troubled. (Ps 6.1ff.)

And in congregations how often the prayer is appropriate:

> Lord, thou hast been our dwelling place in all generations.

Before the mountains were brought forth,
or ever thou hadst formed the earth and the world,
from everlasting to everlasting thou art God. (Ps 90.1f)

It is wonderful how many of the psalms of lament which cry out or scold emerge from the lament mode to full-hearted praise later on in the same psalm.

There is no better example than Ps 22 which begins, "My God, my God, why have you forsaken me?" which is a lament or a complaint against God, but which comes round to,

All the ends of the earth shall remember and turn to the Lord;
and all the families of the nations shall worship before him! (v. 27)

Within the general Lament type the Penitential Psalms are the best known. The most famous of all is Psalm 51.

Have mercy on me, O God, according to thy steadfast love;
According to thy abundant mercy blot out my transgressions.
Wash me thoroughly from my iniquity, and cleanse me from my sin!
For I know my transgressions, and my sin is ever before me.
Against thee, thee only, have I sinned?
And done that which is evil in thy sight,
so thou art justified in thy sentence
and blameless in thy judgment Ps. 51.1ff.

In the penitential psalms the enemy is sometimes outside the worshipper and sometimes within.[7] An example of an enemy within is Ps. 51.10.

Create in me a clean heart O God, and put a new and right spirit within me.

whereas in Ps. 6.8 the enemy is without.

---

[7]. Although penitence is not equally evident in all of them' six psalms have been recognized by Christians as the penitential group - these are 6, 32, 38, 51, 102 and 130, and B. W. Anderson (1983) would add also Ps. 143, (*Out of the Depths,* p. 236).

Depart from me, all you workers of evil;
for the Lord has heard the sound of my weeping.

The *Cursing psalms* have always created problems for believers, both Jewish and Christian. They often present cruel and spiteful sentiments, and they are often full of hatred. There may be no fully satisfying answer but three things may be helpfully said

- Firstly, the psalmists take sin very seriously, and are resolute in condemning those who ignore or compromise with sin. Ps.139.21 asks, "Do I not hate them that hate thee, O Lord?" The inference clearly being that the suppliant must not tolerate or associate with sin even though it will make for a quieter life.

- Secondly, the hatred in these verses can be understood as a response to the total righteousness of God. It is no accident that, of all the literature of the Ancient Near East, that of Israel takes sin most seriously and calls down vengeance upon evil doers with most passion. It is not necessarily that the Jews were greater sinners but perhaps because they took sin so seriously. No other nation ascribed to its God such righteousness as Yahweh had revealed to Israel.

- Finally, often the vagueness and facelessness with which the enemies are described may render us powerless to determine the original context, but for that very reason continue to render these psalms of great use in many situations. We also need to appreciate that the hatred these psalms so honestly portray may not be the way we like to think we behave, but perhaps from time to time this is the pictures of our inner selves. The anonymity of the enemies renders these psalms still appropriate. Because it is almost impossible to exactly determine the original usage or motivation, the psalms are widely and generally applicable to many real-life situations.

Readers will undoubtedly feel at times that they cannot utter these curses against God or enemies or indeed against the forces of evil within ourselves for we know that we are not without sin. It is at such times that it may be helpful to hear these words as if spoken by Jesus, for only Jesus is righteous enough to be able to express such sentiments

4.2 Praises and related types

There are also about 60 psalms of praise. Many of these psalms use the word *Bless*, very often with reference to God, for example, Psalm 103.1, 2, 20, 21,22. The words *thanks* and *thanksgiving* are used less often, but in fact the words have very similar meanings. To bless God and to thank God are the twin and related subjects of these psalms. They are the good responses of the Christian believer, as they were of the Jew before him, to the love and providence of God. Some of the best-known hymns of praise and thanksgiving include Ps. 21 and 116. This latter ends with these words:

> I will offer to thee the sacrifice of thanksgiving
> and call on the name of the Lord.
> I will pay my vows to the Lord
> in the presence of all his people,
> in the courts of the house of the Lord,
> in your midst, O Jerusalem.
> Praise the Lord! Ps. 116.17-19.

Among the Praise Psalms are those psalms recognising God as both Creator and Redeemer, including Ps. 6, 8, 100, 103, 113 and 117.

> O Lord our Lord,
> how majestic is thy name in all the earth!
> Thou whose glory above the heavens is chanted
> by the mouths of babes and infants,
> thou hast founded a bulwark because of thy foes,
> to still the enemy and the avenger. Ps. 8.1-2.

Claus Westermann (1981), while confined in a Prisoner of War camp in the middle of the 20th C., wrote about the psalms of Praise and suggested a fresh approach to the sub-divisions. For him there were declarative psalms where the worshippers directly thanked God for specific acts of deliverance or love, and also descriptive psalms where God is described as praiseworthy. He then identified a series of sub groups such as creation psalms, enthronement psalms, psalms of Zion, and psalms of trust, of which Ps 23 is the classic example.

A section within the general group of praise psalms are the fifteen Songs of Ascent, Psalms 120-134, which may originally have been sung as pilgrims journeyed to Jerusalem. The beautiful One Hundred and Twenty First Psalm is a good example,

I lift up my eyes to the hills.
From whence does my help come?
My help comes from the Lord,
Who made heaven and earth. (Ps. 121.1)

This psalm is also a psalm of trust as well as being in the ancient group of Songs of Ascent.

Finally, there are the Songs of Trust which include some of the best known and most loved of all the Praise psalms. Ps. 23 and 46 are two psalms to which millions in distress turn and find comfort. The Lord is my shepherd (Ps 23) and God is our refuge and strength (Ps 46).

4.3 Royal Psalms.

There are at least eleven of these: Ps 2, 18, 20, 21, 45, 72, 89, 101, 110, 122, and 144. These are all concerned with the ruling kings of Israel of the Davidic line and there are other psalms dealing with God as supreme King. Many of the Royal Psalms suggest to Christian readers a messianic message. Not only in the Royal Psalms but throughout the Psalter there are many psalms which may be interpreted messianically. Thus, it is that these Royal Psalms and Psalms about God as king have lent themselves most easily to a messianic interpretation, and many of them are quoted in the Gospels and the New Testament.

4.4 Wisdom Psalms.

There are also at least 11 Wisdom Psalms although there are other psalms with clear evidence of Wisdom influence. They are Ps 1, 32, 37, 49, 73, 78, 112, 110, 127, 128 and 133. The Wisdom movement in Israel was part of an international movement. There were Wise men throughout the Ancient Near East and for Israel this represented their dialogue with the wider world. In Israel, there were three categories of religious leaders, prophets, priests and wise men. Each of these three categories made their intellectual and religious contribution to the life of the nation. (In later days when the Wise men from the East came to pay homage to the infant Christ that would be an instance of the internationality of the Wisdom movement). The Wisdom psalms are a small group of psalms reflecting that aspect of Israel's life which set out the *sensible* way to live, in harmony with all, giving reason its right place, along with a proper trust in God. The two best known examples are Psalms 37 and 73. These psalms sound very much like the Book of Proverbs, which is the major Wisdom book in the Old Testament

The wicked draw their sword and bend their bow, to bring down the poor and needy,
To slay those who walk uprightly;
Their sword shall enter their own heart, and their bows shall be broken. (Ps. 37.14-15)
a very present help in trouble.
Therefore we will not fear though the earth should change,
though the mountains shake in the heart of the sea;
though its waters roar and foam,
though the mountains tremble with its tumult. Ps. 46.1-3.

As noted above, it is often not immediately apparent to which type a psalm belongs as so many exhibit the characteristics of more than one type. Many psalms can easily be identified as belonging to one of several groups, for it is common for psalms to sound more than one note. It is only with practice that the reader begins to be conscious of the dominant message of a particular psalm. Here Ps 46 exhibits some Wisdom characteristics.

5. Law and Judgement

Law in the modern world is understood as the authoritative force necessary for the maintenance of civil and community order, in contrast to law in Old Testament Times where law is a positive concept to be equated with God's will. We need to accept a different understanding of *Law* when reading the Old Testament in order to appreciate how the children of Israel viewed their Law. For them it was one of the most precious and wonderful gifts that God had ever showered upon them. It formed the basis of a properly ordered life where relationships between God and the people were as God intended. So, the Psalmist could describe law as "sweeter than honey," and as "more to be desired than gold" (Ps. 19.10). This understanding of God's Law, not as a force bearing down and liable to oppress people but as a liberating and redeeming way to live in accordance with the will of God, is what

Christians need and is how the Psalmists under-stand the Law. An example of this is the cleansing power of the Law as one of the components of Psalm 19 where the sun becomes an image of the scorching cleansing power that the Law has.

It's [the sun's] rising is from the ends of the heavens,
and its circuit to the end of them;
and there is nothing hid from its heat. (Ps. 19.6)
Psalm 19 contains some of the most powerful statements of the beauty of the Law of the Lord:
The Law of the Lord is perfect, reviving the soul;
the testimony of the Lord is sure, making wise the simple;
the precepts of the Lord are right, rejoicing the heart;
the commandment of the Lord is pure, enlightening the eyes;
the fear of the Lord is clean, enduring for ever;
the ordinances of the Lord are true, and righteous altogether.
More to be desired are they than gold, even much fine gold;
sweeter also than honey, and drippings of the honeycomb. (Ps. 19.7-10)

Psalms of judgment like Ps. 35 allow us to see that, while a Christian trembles at the thought of judgment, a Jew looks forward to it. C.S. Lewis (1958) points out that, whereas the Jew sees himself as a plaintiff seeking damages, the Christian only sees himself as a defendant looking for acquittal. Christians want mercy not justice.[8]

6 Festival songs and liturgies

Although not specifically a separate type, there are very many psalms which seem likely to have been sung at great annual festivals, such as the Passover, the Feast of Pentecost, the Feast of Tab-ernacles, the occasion of annual Covenant Renewal, when Israel remembered that God was the enthroned King of Kings. These are also the psalms that deal with the relationship between Yahweh and the human kings of Israel. In this group are also the psalms that speak of Jerusalem and Zion as the earthly dwelling place of God.

[8.] C.S Lewis (1958) Reflections on the Psalms pg. 10 Geoffrey Bles London

The search for a satisfying classification into psalm types has been an important aspect of psalm study over the past 100 years. So too is the related topic of associating given psalms with occasions in the religious life of the children of Israel. Estimates have varied greatly in the number of psalms which can be designated to any of the festivals or annual occasions. Some psalms have been called Enthronement Psalms, because they clearly would have been appropriate for such an occasion, when either the Enthronement of Yahweh as Israel's Sovereign Lord was celebrated or when a human king was enthroned as the king of Israel or Judah (Bellinger WH 2012). It is not surprising that there have been considerable variations in the suggested psalms when we think of the large number of contemporary hymns which can be sung quite appropriately on many different occasions. Typical Enthronement psalms will be Psalms 81 and 96.

O sing to the Lord a new song;
sing to the Lord, all the earth!
Sing to the Lord, bless his name;
tell of his salvation from day to day. (Ps. 96.1-2)

Whereas this would be appropriate at an Enthronement occasion, it would also be appropriate at a Covenant Renewal Festival, or indeed at many celebrations and other commitment occasions. So too Ps. 81.1f.

Sing aloud to God our strength;
shout for joy to the God of Jacob!
Raise a song, sound the timbrel,
the sweet lyre with the harp.

What is indisputable is that Israel had many occasions for celebration, and many of the psalms would have been appropriate at these functions. That we can continue to use them to celebrate the love and majesty, the forgiveness and compassion of the God and Father of our Lord Jesus Christ, strengthens our conviction of the continuity of the faith from Abraham even till today.

7. Reading Psalms and Asking Questions

The study of psalms is concerned with asking questions of psalm type, purpose, date, meaning and authorship, though not all of these are appropriate for every psalm. While the original historical situation of a great many of the psalms is no longer apparent or significant, there are exceptions and Ps 137, which refers to life in Babylon, is one of them.

Students, ministers and Bible study leaders will have their own particular questions. For some, what did a psalm mean to the Psalmist and those who first heard it, and what does it mean now? For others, was it written by an individual out of the depths of his own experience and subsequently used by others, or was it written by one of the Temple musicians or priests for worshippers either individually or as a congregation? For many the crucial questions will be to ask what does this psalm tell us about God and our relationship to Him? For personal study the absolutely vital question is, how might a psalm change me?

It is now generally held that the majority of the psalms reached their final form at the hands of Temple officials in order to meet the needs of the worshipping congregation in all the different aspects of worship. Nevertheless, this does not exclude the affirmation that many of the psalms are very old and that many different people will have written them, including King David. C.S. Lewis (1958) reminds his readers that, while nowadays artists apparently can only create great works in moments of inspiration, such has not always been the case.[9]

It is useful to be able to distinguish between the private psalms and the more public ones; those written for individuals and those written with a more congregational use in mind. Christians will also want to know whether or not there is a specifically Christian understanding of the psalm in addition to the Jewish interpretation. One very interesting aspect of the privacy or otherwise of a psalm is to ask how many people, or groups of people are involved in it? Two examples will show some of the contrasts: Psalm 139, which is a most private prayer where the suppliant pours out his soul, only involves the suppliant, the Lord, and in the final, verses the hated enemy. In contrast, is Psalm 22 which is public, involving the suppliant, God, "our fathers", good and bad men, the congregation, and as is very often the case, mention is also made of his mother. Once again, the whole Psalter is seen both as Hymn Book and Prayer Book for Jews and Christians.

Enough has now been said in the last two chapters to show that many questions can be asked, both about each separate psalm and about all of them as a collection.

When reading a psalm, only a limited number of questions can be in

---

[9.] C.S Lewis (1958) Reflections on the Psalms Geoffrey Bles London our minds at any one time. For this reason, it is necessary to be prepared to read each psalm often in order to put all the questions that are to be asked, and even then, to realise that, when all the questions have been asked, our knowledge will still be incomplete. We are removed from all of these psalms by time, by culture and by the Cross of Christ. Tremper Longman (1988) uses the analogy that we are separated by various kinds of distance from the original psalms and their writers which changes our perspective as there was little expectation of heaven.[10]

With the Bible open and a notebook ready, the process can begin. A psalm is selected for exploration and investigation. It is profitable to read it a number of times, each time asking one or more different questions.

At the first reading we can identify some of the divisions into strophes. These sense units are easily discernible in most psalms. At the beginning of this chapter, for example, the first verses of Ps. 103 form one of the four main sections of the psalm.

At a second reading we might ask ourselves about the psalm type, and its possible original use in the Temple at Jerusalem. That would lead us naturally to consider when we would use such a psalm nowadays. Ps 103 has been described as a Hymn of Praise and would have had as many uses in the Temple as it does in contemporary Christian worship.

Reading philosophy encourages the same process, asking if this theory is consistent with life and practical experience. So too for an instruction booklet on how to do or make something, in which the reader will be inquiring, and will work out how is it done. The appropriate questions to ask are easily identified in each case and the book fulfils its purpose. So too, when reading a psalm, there are these appropriate questions to ask in order to establish the context and explore the meaning.

At the next reading the date may perhaps be guessed at, and whether there are any indications from language or style or vocabulary to point towards the monarchy, the exile in Babylon or after the return from exile?

A further reading can be with the purpose of relating the psalm to Jesus. The reader can imagine that Jesus is alongside and listening to his rendering of the psalm. This approach will be explored further in

---

[10.] Tremper Longman (1988) How to Read the Psalms Leicester Inter Varsity Press pg. 13-14

chapter 5.

Finally, having prepared well and having sought what the psalm may have meant in the past, it is appropriate to ask what it means now. All the previous readings will have informed this final reading. At this point the devotional, the pastoral and the academic needs of the reader come together.

8. Some of the challenges facing the reader:

1. Every psalm is different and not all are collected into easily recognizable groups of related psalms.

2. To enter the world of a new psalm and to get on to its wavelength is seldom a quick or easy process.

3. They were written centuries ago, by people in the Middle East, in situations very different from anything in many affluent countries today. They are about entering a Promised Land and offering animal sacrifices upon a stone altar, and yet they strike a chord and have done so for thousands of years!

4. Today the psalms are read as those living after Christ, and so read after Jesus had read them. Christians will want to read many psalms messianically and see the advent of the Messiah which is foretold in the psalms being fulfilled in the person of Christ the Messiah.

5. How do Christians believe that the psalms be read alongside Jesus? How would, or how did, Jesus read and understand the psalms?

6. When reading the cursing psalms, how ought they to be handled, aware that Christians are not to malign lightly or indeed to curse and wish ill on others?

The psalms have tutored Christian believers both in private prayers and in communal worship. Behind, in and through the ancient words, the Church has found the promptings of the Spirit of God."[11]

To gradually understand the psalms will allow the reader to have the

---

[11] W. S. McCullough and W.R. Taylor (1955), *Interpreters' Bible Vol 4,* New York: Abingdon, pp. 16-17.

appropriate psalm or verse for a wide variety of situations. As they get to know them better, the words will come into their lives.

DISCUSSION TOPICS

1. What is the significance of the different words for God used in the Book of Psalms?

2. How can the reader relate to the different world order in time and place that produced the psalms?

CHAPTER THREE

PSALMS FOR ALL SITUATIONS

For Sadness, for Sickness, for Celebration

In 2003 *Psalms for Sadness Sickness and Celebration* was published (Gordon R 2003). In this small book, twenty of the shortest psalms were selected and each was illustrated with a photograph. Appended to the text of each psalm was a short prayer. Surprisingly the book went to three editions within five years. Simplicity and brevity were its strengths. Included were praise psalms, lament psalms, royal psalms and wisdom psalms, representatives of the four major types of psalms.

There are psalms for all seasons and all occasions. Some of the best known are widely used in a great variety of occasions. Psalm 23 is used in individual and public worship, at funerals, weddings and countless other gatherings. Psalms are sung at Christian harvest celebrations, e.g. Ps 6, reminding the reader that the original use of many psalms was for the great annual occasions in Jewish worship including harvest. Ps 6 is a highly personal psalm to meditate upon:

O Lord, rebuke me not in thy anger,
nor chasten me in thy wrath.
Be gracious to me, O Lord, for I am languishing;
O Lord, heal me, for my bones are troubled.
But thou, O Lord - how long?
Turn, O Lord, save my life; deliver me for the sake of thy steadfast love.
For in death there is no remembrance of thee; in Sheol,
who can give thee praise?
I am weary with my moaning; every night I flood my bed with tears;
I drench my couch with my weeping.
My eye wastes because of my grief, it grows weak because of all my foes.
Depart from me, all you workers of evil for the Lord has heard the sound of my weeping.
The Lord has heard my supplication; the Lord accepts my prayer.
All my enemies shall be ashamed and sorely troubled;

they shall turn back, and be put to shame in a moment.

It is self-evident that the psalms are able to comfort the distressed, bring relief to the burdened, help the happy to sing, and that they are able to meet every emotional need. For thousands of years' believers have given their testimony that the psalms have expressed their feelings and allowed them to communicate with God in every physical, emotional and spiritual situation. The aim of this chapter is much more modest, and is simply to illustrate some of the situations for which there are appropriate psalms. By so doing the believer will be encouraged to know the Psalter well enough to find the right psalm for every moment.

In common with much of the Bible, many psalms can serve as 'mirrors for our souls.' This has been known for centuries and many famous writers on the psalms have drawn attention to this. John Calvin, writing about the psalms in the 16th C could say; "I have been accustomed to call this book, I think not inappropriately, 'An anatomy of all parts of the soul'; for there is not an emotion of which any one can be conscious that is not represented here as in a mirror."[12]

Contemporary writers on the psalms still do so, and the psalms are not alone in this, for the earlier chapters of Genesis, among other Bible chapters, can also hold a mirror before our souls.

In this chapter examples are given where the psalmist is sometimes downcast, sometimes happy, sometimes sad, and sometimes even mad with rage. This will challenge readers to identify their moods with those of the psalmist.

There are psalms for good and for bad behaviour. Some messianic psalms also direct the reader towards Jesus Christ who is good beyond human standards. Particularly in the psalms which speak of an impossibly wonderful king, and a long-awaited Messiah and speak of a king or a messiah with such qualities that no human monarch will ever fulfil. Christian readers of the psalms can realise that only Jesus could fulfil such and these psalms are messianic where the Messiah, an anointed one, comes to deliver Israel, is divine and not merely a human redeemer for Israel. There are other psalms which curse and scold in ways which offend and embarrass us. They are more easily understood with Jesus alongside for only He is good enough to justifiably feel such

---

[12]. "Mirror of the soul" The idea apparently was first used by John Calvin in the 16th C and later by Kahil Gibran (1979) as the title of his famous book Mirrors of the Soul.

emotions. We shall return to these two aspects of the psalms in Chapter 6.

Many of these are in the singular person, but with the recognition that they will also be used by a congregation. Psalm 23 is a good example:

"The Lord is **my** shepherd," is also universally understood to mean: "The Lord is **our** shepherd."

Another favourite psalm for congregational or community use is Psalm 121 with the opening question:

I lift my eyes to the hills.
From where does my help come?

This again is written in the singular but has clearly met congregational needs whenever it has been used. When we say or sing this psalm in public worship we understand it in the plural:

Where does *our* help come from when we lift *our* eyes to the hills? Our help comes from the Sovereign Lord. (and not from the hills, which was where the Canaanites had their high or holy places where they worshipped Baal). Presumably, any congregation singing any psalm identifies it in the plural.

There is the large group of psalms which have been identified as psalms of individual lament, numbering about 45. For not only are they written in the singular person but many of these seem to be much more personal, and whereas they may have had some Temple use, and indeed they may also be used in a congregational setting, nevertheless they seem more fitted for private devotion. It is this group which supplies the largest numbers of soul mirrors for many human emotions. These Individual Laments are found throughout the Psalter but more of them in Books I and II (Psalms 1-72). There are also a small number of individual psalms of thanksgiving (perhaps 8 of them).

It is intriguing to wonder why there is more lament than thanksgiving. One possibility is that, throughout the Bible, the moral leaders such as the law-givers, the prophets, the priests and the wise men have more often identified the sins of Israelites and condemned the children of Israel for them, than they have ever given praise to Israel.

34

The same is true of the Book of Psalms. There is less commendation for the Israelites for good behaviour, than the many times Israel is taken to task for her individual or collective sins.

For an individual and for a congregation there are appropriate psalms for every occasion and for all our felt emotions. When there is sickness or sadness, joy or success, there is an appropriate word from the psalms, which allows believers the opportunity to relate their emotions to God. Appended is a list of twelve of life's emotions and traumas, and with each, references to some psalms to which one might turn. This list is neither complete nor will it be the only list. Ideally each psalm reader needs to compile their own personal list of those psalms which have mirrored their souls in their different moods and to which reference can be made as need arises.

1. Grief: Psalms 31.9; 6.6-7,
2. Anger: Psalms 4.4; 76.10,
3. Sickness and pain: Psalms 103.1ff., 13.2,
4. Despair: Psalms 42 and 43,
5. Revenge: Psalms 17.13f; 18.4-42; 109.3-19,
6. Confession: Psalms 32, 51,102 130, 143,
7. Fear : Psalms. 34.4f 22.1; 22.19-21; 56.3-4,
8. Doubt: Psalms 37, 49, 73, and 133,
9. Need: Psalms 40.1-10, 46,
10. Worry: Psalms 42, 43; 116 and 118,
11. Joy: Psalm 16 especially verses 5-11, Psalms 84 and 96-99,
12. Affirming faith and expressing trust: Psalms 23, 27.1-6; 91; 121.

1. Grief: Psalms 31.9; 6.6-7

Be gracious to me, O Lord, for I am in distress;
my eye is wasted from grief,
my soul and my body also. (Ps. 31.9)
I am weary with my moaning;
every night I flood my bed with tears;
I drench my couch with my weeping.
My eye wastes away because of grief,
it grows weak because of all my foes. (Ps. 6.6-7)

The reader is not told what the original trauma that led the psalmist to write these verses was. The psalmist may have known from personal experience that this was a universal circumstance that anyone may have to endure at any time and everyone will at some time have to suffer.

Psalm 31 speaks of intense suffering. Body, eye and soul are all sick with sadness. The sufferer feels the scorn of enemies, knows the pain of being deserted by friends and has the disturbing feeling that people are talking about him.

Imagine the grief of a young Kenyan theological student in 1975 when he and his equally young wife lost their first baby. The sad little funeral was devastating and there was great need at such a time to be able to say.

> But I trust in thee, O Lord,
> I say, "Thou art my God."
> My times are in His hand. (Ps. 31.14-15)

Forty-five years later the same couple have raised a lovely family and have known a worthwhile ministry in the Presbyterian Church of East Africa.

2. Anger: Psalm 4.4

Anger is expressed in the psalms: It can sometimes be the quiet controlled anger that the psalmist seems to allow as in 4.4:

> Be angry, but sin not;
> Commune with your own hearts on your bed,
> and be silent.

It may be the anger of the psalmist's enemies

> Attend to me, and answer me; I am distraught by the noise of the enemy,
> Because of the oppression of the wicked.
> For they bring trouble upon me,
> And in anger they cherish enmity against me. (Ps. 55.2-3)

Very much more often it is the anger of God, e.g. Psalms. 6.1f, 7.6, 30.5; 38.1; 69.24; 80.4

Arise, O Lord, in thy anger,
Lift thyself against the fury of my enemies; awake,
O my God; thou hast appointed a judgment. Psalm 7.6

Many have felt, with Job, that there is a place for righteous indignation and at times we feel that we can justify our bad temper and our cross words.

Job opened his mouth and cursed the day of his birth. (Job 3.1).

and so too did Jeremiah in a well-known passage:

Cursed be the day on which I was born!
Why did I come forth from the womb, to see toil and sorrow,
And spend my days in shame? (Jeremiah 20.14-18)

For these are surely the words of very angry men?
St. Paul seems to quote Ps. 4.4 positively, "Be angry but sin not …" and uses this as his authority to allow anger, but even there, he warns that it must be short lived:

Do not let the sun go down on your anger. (Ephesians 4.26)

Maybe in Psalm 76.10 there is a justification for some of the anger of men:

Man's wrath only adds to your glory;
the survivors of your wrath you will draw like a girdle around you;
(Ps. 76.10 Jerusalem Bible 1968).

Although the meaning of this verse is difficult, the Jerusalem Bible does make the meaning plainer to justify much human anger!

Therefore, it would seem that there is very little, if any, support for human anger in the psalms. In the great majority of cases where the word anger is used in the psalms it is the anger of God that is the subject. Frequently sinners deserve the wrath of God and it is only in his mercy and goodness that they are spared. The words of Ps. 6.1 are a wonderful balm:

37

O Lord, rebuke me not in thy anger,
Nor chasten me in thy wrath.
Be gracious to me, O Lord, for I am languishing;
O Lord heal me for my bones are troubled.

This all seems to indicate that if we turn to the Book of the Psalms to find excuses for our bad temper we shall look in vain!

3. Sickness and pain: Psalms 103.1ff, 13.2, and 38.

Although sickness and pain are not in themselves emotions, they very often lead to the emotions of fear and worry. There are many passages in the psalms which are very good to turn to in times of sickness. Reading them, or hearing them read or recited can often bring great peace of mind and assurance to both the patient and to the carers.

Ps. 103 is not an Individual Lament and can be accurately described as a hymn for use by a congregation. Yet it has often been read and prayed beside the beds of suffering patients and has brought healing and peace to many deeply troubled sick people.

Bless the Lord, O my soul;
all that is within me,
Bless his holy name!
Bless the Lord, O my soul,
and forget not all his benefits,
who forgives all your iniquities,
who heals all your diseases. (Ps. 103)

There is also a most important link with Psalm 41.1-3

Blessed is he who considers the poor!
The Lord delivers him in the day of trouble;
The Lord sustains him on his sick-bed;
in his illness thou healest all his infirmities. (Ps. 41.3)

For example, cancer is a cruel disease, cruel alike to those who suffer and to those who watch and care. Cancer is no respecter of age or rank there are few who have not been involved. The balm of the words of Psalm 103.1-5 are very powerful. So too are the words of Psalm 84 which can be understood to have a double meaning, for it speaks both of a home on earth and speaks also to Christians, about an eternal dwelling place:

How lovely is thy dwelling place, O Lord of Hosts!
My soul longs, yea faints for the courts of the Lord;
my heart and flesh sing for joy to the living God. (Ps. 84.1-2)

When words like these are read and prayed beside the beds of terminally ill patients, Christ will often be realised in the room and the Word of God ministers with its divine power. When all the human help has been given and all the human words have been spoken then the Silence of the Presence of God can meet the deepest need.

AIDS is still one of the most rapidly spreading diseases in Sub-Saharan Africa, and each case brings great suffering to many others. Widows are left without support, orphans are created, village life is crushed with burdens that are too heavy to carry, and poverty is multiplied. There was no such disease in the times of the psalmists but Psalm 38 verses 17-18 may be appropriate:

For I am ready to fall,
and my pain is ever with me.
I confess my iniquity,
I am sorry for my sin. (Ps. 38.17-18)

Psalm 38 is a very tough psalm. It is both a prayer for healing and a recognition of responsibility.

4. Despair: Psalms 42; 43

Many will never suffer from cancer or AIDS but everyone will from time to time suffer bouts of despair and loneliness. There are simply thousands of situations which can lead to feelings of utter hopelessness. Hunger, money worries, difficult relationships within and outside of families, educational problems, and sheer tiredness are only a few of the causes of despair. It is at these moments that the believer is driven to wonder, 'Has God forgotten me?' At such times, nothing is more beautiful than to behold the face of God:

As a hart longs for flowing streams,
So, longs my soul for thee, O God,
My soul thirsts for God, for the living God.

39

When shall I come and behold the face of God? (Ps. 42.1-2)

Psalms 42 and 43 are a pair of related psalms, which can be read as a single psalm (perhaps they were originally one). There is the thrice repeated agonising question:

Why are you cast down, O my soul,
And why are you disquieted within me? (Ps. 42.11a)

Three times also the psalmist declares with wonderful reassurance:

Hope in God; for I shall again praise him,
My help and my God. (Ps. 42.11b)

This psalm may have been composed during the Babylonian Exile and, if so, will originally have expressed the longing of the psalmist and those for whom he wrote to be able to return to their beloved native land of Judah and to Jerusalem. This same psalm has in the intervening centuries brought comfort and hope to many people.

5. Revenge: Psalms 17.13f; 18.4-42; 109.3-19

The Christian Church has inherited from Judaism the firm conviction that revenge is God's prerogative. When Paul writes in Romans 12.19: "Vengeance is mine", says the Lord;" he is quoting from both Leviticus 19:18 and Deuteronomy 32.35.

Even though Paul's teaching is accepted, angry worshippers can still cry to the Lord for his revenge upon their enemies. We have many biblical precedents calling down divine wrath on those who have hurt us, deceived us, oppressed us or disappointed us. In Psalm 17.13f we can hear again a voice like the voice of a Job crying to God, that He will avenge him of the injustice he has suffered.

Arise, O Lord, confront them, overthrow them!
Deliver my life from the wicked by thy sword,
The psalmist goes on, in verse 14:
May their belly be filled with what thou hast stored up for them;

And the psalmist finishes on a very mild note:

May their children have more than enough.
May they leave something over for their babies.

Other psalms calling for revenge are not so muted. The notorious verses 7-9 in the otherwise beautiful Psalm 137 contain the frightening lines:

Remember, O Lord, against the Edomites
the day of Jerusalem,
how they said, "Raze it, raze it!
Down to its foundations!"
O daughter of Babylon, you devastator!
Happy shall he be who requites you
With what you have done to us!
Happy shall he be who takes your little ones
and dashes them against the rock! (Ps. 137, 7-9)

Psalm 18 is a complicated narrative where the psalmist expresses various emotions. He tells of how he has enjoyed God's protection and there is the lovely line:

He brought me forth into a broad place,
And delivered me,
Because he has delighted in me. (Ps. 18.19)

This expresses the same gratitude and confidence as does Ps. 16.5-6.

You, Lord, are all I have,
and you give me all I need;
my future is in your hands.
How wonderful are your gifts to me,
how good they are!

However, Psalm 18 includes what some will read as a precedent for personal revenge in verses 37-39.

I pursue my enemies and catch them;
I do not stop until I destroy them.
I strike them down, and they cannot rise;
They lie defeated before me.

Yet this psalm has some difficult lines from another angle. Can any one of us can say, as in verse 23:

I was blameless before him,
and I kept myself from guilt. (Good News Bible 2002)

This is a condition experienced by few if any and is only fully true on the lips of Jesus. These thoughts will be taken up again in Chapter 4. Only Jesus was always truly blameless.

6. Confession: Psalms 32; 51; 102; 130; 143.

These five, along with Psalms 6 and 38, comprise the group which has been called by Christians the Seven Penitential psalms. When a believer is overcome with guilt he can turn to these wonderfully therapeutic lines and make confession of sin. Because everyone feels guilty from time to time, the very act of the acknowledgement of sin is
in itself good, and these are the psalms to which every believer can turn. Ps 32.5

I acknowledged my sin to thee, and I did not hide my iniquity;
I said, "I will confess my transgressions to the Lord";
then thou didst forgive the guilt of my sin.

Although the Old Testament cannot reach the certainty and the wholeness of the personal forgiveness declared by Jesus, the psalmists time after time declare the power and willingness of God to forgive sin. Psalm 51 is the most direct statement of this forgiveness, and how we repeatedly need the reassurance of its words:

Have mercy upon me, O God, according to thy steadfast love;
According to thy abundant mercy
Blot out my transgressions. (Ps. 51.1)

and

Purge me with hyssop, and I shall be clean;
wash me and I shall be whiter than snow. (Ps. 51.7)

These are both a declaration of forgiveness for the penitent sinner and a clear preparation for the fuller development of this teaching in the New Testament. Indeed, we cannot claim to fully understand the forgiveness declared by Jesus in the New Testament unless we know something of the teaching of the Old Testament upon which He built.

This illustrates the more general truth that the New Testament is only fully understandable in the light and the teaching of the Old Testament.

For a final example the beautiful simplicity of Psalm 38.18 expresses the penitence and the humility with which we now, as they then, need to come to the throne of grace, "I confess my iniquity, I am sorry for my sin."

7. Fear: Psalms 34.4f; 22.19-21; 56.3-4; 46.1ff

Fear is one of life's most disturbing emotions. It is eternally reassuring to remember the long record of frightened martyrs who have gone willingly to their deaths with the words of psalms on their lips. Every century has produced inspiring examples and perhaps Dietrich Bonhoeffer, who was executed by the Nazi regime in 1945, is an outstanding example in the twentieth century. His dependence upon the word of God, the intensity with which he came to the whole Bible including the Book of Psalms, while in detention, has moved many a lesser disciple who has read his account of those months and years (Bonhoeffer D 1953).

The young Ugandan martyrs executed by the Kabaka in the nineteenth century were another group of faithful warriors for Christ who gave their lives for what they believed, and their last words too may have been some like:

I sought the Lord, and he answered me, and delivered me from all my fears. (Ps. 34.4)

This line has been the prayer, and the proclamation, of unnumbered believers since ever it was written.

The cry of the psalmist which Jesus made His own from Psalm 22 is well known:

My God, my God, why hast thou forsaken me?

This may or may not have been an expression of fear by Jesus, but has, when used by others, often expressed terrifying fear of being alone without God. This same psalm comes around to the powerful remedy.

But thou, O Lord, be not afar off!
O thou my help, hasten to my aid!
Deliver my soul from the sword,
my life from the power of the dog!
Save me from the mouth of the lion,
my afflicted soul from the horns of the wild oxen! (Ps. 22.19-21)

Many people will have good reasons to be thankful for these not so well known verses from Psalm 56.3-4:

When I am afraid, I put my trust in thee.
In God, whose word I praise,
in God, I trust without a fear.
What can flesh do to me?

It is possible that this line from Psalm 56 may have inspired the very much better known New Testament texts in Matthew 10.26-31 and Philippians 4.4-7.

And do not fear those who kill the body but cannot kill the soul. (Mt 10.28.)
Have no anxiety about anything, but in everything by prayer and supplication
With thanksgiving let your requests be made known to God. (Phil 4.6)

The fear we feel when we are frightened has always got to be distinguished from the fear of the Lord, which is a different idea altogether. Christians like everyone else will at times be frightened but they have One to whom they may turn and will often have need to turn, e.g. Ps. 46.1 'God is our refuge and strength, a very present help in trouble.'

8. Doubt: Psalms 37; 49; 73; 133

Doubt is a difficult emotion to deal with. It plagued the prophet Jeremiah, had troubled believers before him and has done ever since. Jeremiah's confessions include this verse:

44

Why does the way of the wicked prosper? Why do all who are treacherous thrive? (Jer. 12.1)

This same doubt plagues the psalmist who wrote Psalm 37.1

Fret not yourself because of the wicked, be not envious of wrong doers!"

In the same psalm the answer is provided:

But the meek shall possess the land, and delight themselves in abundant prosperity (Ps. 37.11)

Here is a further instance where we can appreciate how the psalms have influenced the New Testament for clearly this verse anticipates the Beatitudes in Matthew 5.1-3, 5.

In a very different way Psalm 133 may well be born out of a situation of doubt about relationships within a family when brothers do not dwell in unity. It is the deep longing of the psalmist that relationships within the family should be good and the deeply emotional words of this little psalm will have been echoed by countless families ever since:

Behold, how good and pleasant it is when brothers dwell in unity!
It is like the precious oil upon the head, running down upon the beard.
For there the Lord has commanded the blessing, life for evermore.

9. Need: Psalms 40.1-10; 46.

Need is one of the most frequently experienced emotions. It may be physical, intellectual or spiritual or any combination of these. Can any believer go through even one day without being conscious of the need of God? We are aware that some of our needs are trivial and we are almost ashamed to bring them before our Heavenly Father, when we see how they compare with the much greater needs of others.

Malawi, for example, is not the only country where there are the hungry months every year as the new crops mature. How can the well-off be excused any self-pity or moaning in the face of so much obvious physical pain and need being experienced by the tens of thousands of poor throughout every one of those hungry days? But it is the need of which anyone is conscious of at a particular moment which is uppermost in their own mind. When an individual is hungry it is their hunger that gnaws at their stomach, when disappointed in love, it is their heart that is near breaking point, when anyone seems to be without a friend in the world it is their need of fellowship which pains them, when anyone sick or in pain they may know with their minds that others are worse off, but they have to cope with their own trials. In all these situations, it is again Ps. 46.1, and 10 which are unsurpassed.

God is our refuge and strength, a very present help in trouble.
Therefore, we will not fear, though the earth should change,
though the mountains shake in the midst of the sea;
Be still and know that I am God. (Ps 46.10).

Psalm. 103 has already been cited as a help in the specific case of sickness and pain, but is also a blessing in many other situations of need.

As a father has compassion on his children,
so the Lord has compassion on those who fear him. (Ps. 103.13)
(NIV 1966)

10. Worry: Psalms 42/43; 116; 118

Psalms about worry offer Christians some coping strategies. Worries can be real or imaginary, and whichever they are, they are frightening and depressing. Ps 42/43 remain one of the most emotional psalms in the entire collection, and have great potential to calm troubled souls. They may not solve the worry nor make it vanish but such passages will allow the worry to take its rightful place in their legitimate concerns and will reassure them that God is in charge. These two verses from Psalm 118 have helped many trouble souls:

This is the day which the Lord has made;
let us rejoice and be glad in it.
Save us, we beseech thee, O Lord!
O Lord, we beseech thee, give us success! (Ps. 118. 24-25)

and also, these verses:

I love the Lord, because he has heard
my voice and my supplications.
Because he inclined his ear to me,
therefore, I will call on him as long as I live. (Ps. 116.1-2)

11. Joy: Psalm 16: 5-11; 84; 96; 97; 98; 99

These psalms along with others are thought by many to have originated
as psalms celebrating the Annual Enthronement of God as the Sovereign
Lord of the universe. They have gone on to serve in the role of being
vehicles for expressing the joy and gratitude of believers in every
imaginable situation where the faithful want and need to give thanks to
God for all his goodness. Psalm 16.6 (GNB 1968) says:

How wonderful are your gifts to me; how good they are! cf. also Ps.
18.19

and Ps. 16.9

And so, I am thankful and glad
and I feel completely secure.

Here is the expressed emotion that God is good and we are prepared to
acknowledge his goodness.

Psalm 84 may have been sung originally by pilgrims going up to the
city of Jerusalem to observe one or other of the three great festivals at
which all males were required to attend annually. Many women also
went, though their going was not enforced by law. It is a song you
would sing while on a journey, perhaps a journey to Jerusalem. Ever
since, this psalm has been understood by many Jews and Christians as
the life's journey upon which all believers are engaged, the journey of
faith and pilgrimage from now until eternity. For countless numbers this
psalm has expressed the joy experienced by believers as they went on
with God. There is the joy of the journey and there is the anticipated
fuller joy, which Christians reading the psalm will understand, as that
full communion with our Lord which will be ours in the fullness of time.

12. Affirming faith and expressing trust: Psalms 23; 27.1-6; 91; 121

When there is need to affirm faith, there are the famous psalms of trust and confidence like. Psalms 23, 27.1-6, 91 and 121. These are among the best known of all psalms and cannot be limited in their identification as communal or individual for they speak to everyone and for everyone, whether alone or in the company of a worshipping congregation. These psalms have a very wide range of situations where they are applicable and appropriate. Psalm 23 is sung at baptisms, weddings and funerals, and is also recited in the quiet of the night by the grateful mother who has just given birth to her first child, as it is also said by the saddened man who has just seen his mother's eyes close in death. Both Psalms 23 and 121 have been prayed in joy and sorrow, in sickness and health and in thousands of other situations so numerous that they cannot be numbered:

> The Lord will keep you from all evil; he will keep your life.
> The Lord will keep your going out and your coming in
> from this time forth and for evermore. (Ps. 121.7-8)

The psalmist had in mind God the Father Almighty, and when we who are in Christ pray and say and sing those words, we address them to our Lord and Saviour Jesus Christ.

DISCUSSION TOPICS

1. How can a psalm be a 'mirror of the soul?'

2. What psalm would you offer to someone in great need? Why?

48

CHAPTER FOUR

PSALMS FOR FUNERALS AND WEDDINGS

FUNERALS

Christians read the psalms looking for, and finding, words and thoughts that are fulfilled in Christ. They find comfort and strength, a guiding hand and a leading light when they are uncertain and distressed. So it is, time and time again at funerals, and in churches, and by open graves, that the psalms have brought to us the power and the presence of God. Believers have been able to rise above the trouble and uncertainty of mourning and glimpse the eternal shore.

In the words of some of the psalms there is an awareness of death, an appreciation of the shortness of life, an assurance of the nearness of God, and an expression of the certainty of his love which makes them an essential part of the liturgy of departure for believers. Funerals can be the beginning of a new and better life for all who are in Christ. Christian funerals mark a new beginning and not merely an end of life!

God is so good! Following Christ's gracious invitation to faith God allows every Christian disciple the rest of their life, however short or long that may be, to practise the presence of God. That presence is often vividly real at moments of crisis and trauma. At these times the remembered phrases from familiar psalms, along with words that make their impact for the first time from new psalms, are as precious to believers as nuggets of gold to a prospector, or water to a thirsty traveller in a sun-drenched barren land.

This need not surprise us when we remember that the psalms were written to provide proper vehicles for needy worshippers in every possible human drama. Christians have taken the pre-Christian words and brought to them the rich promises of Christ.

It will be helpful to see if we can discover the reasons why some of these songs have spoken to mourning people with such power and comfort. As far as is known none of the psalms were designated as being specifically appropriate for funerals or mourning situations. But there are perhaps six psalms which have brought most comfort to millions in bereavement situations (Ps 16,23,84,90,103, and 121). It will be valuable to try to discover some of the features which render them particularly suitable for people suffering loss.

Psalms 16, 23, and 121 have much in common. All three are written in the first person singular and, although they are often used for corporate worship, their appeal is that, even when we sing them or hear then in a congregation, we can so readily apply the words personally.

Psalm 16 Preserve me O God, for in thee I take refuge

Psalm 16 is a prayer to God and a song about God. In grief situations, there can be few words which bring more comfort. The psalm could be entitled "Living with God." At several points, this psalm can be seen as the anticipation of Christian thought about life after death. Sheol and the pit (v.10)[13] are not in this context seen as the final abode of the believer, and in the final verse Christians will easily understand the words as applicable to the fullness of the Gospel of Christ "in my presence there is fullness of joy". Philippians 1.23 comes easily to mind: "Better far to be with Christ."

In this powerful psalm the passing and the permanent, the false and the true, the absence and the presence of God are set side by side in stark contrast. The words have the power to bring relief, reassurance and hope to those who grieve. These are good words and good thoughts to have about you at a funeral. In an age of uncertainty and disbelief this psalm also makes a very clear faith statement. This is what we believe and many have stood on this firm ground for many centuries!

Psalms 23 *The Lord is my shepherd*

So much has been written about the Twenty Third Psalm that it is well-nigh impossible to say anything that has not been said. It is nevertheless necessary, however, to record that this is the psalm that has more applications than any other. It has been noted many times that here is the psalm that is equally applicable to grief and joy, to celebration and to

---

[13] There are many synonyms for the word 'hell' in the various English translations of the book of Psalms. The majority are translations of the Hebrew word 'Sheol'. The word itself can be variously understood in the book of Psalms.
The New Testament writers translated the Hebrew 'Sheol' into the Greek 'Hades' and the Christian understanding of hell is a state of alienation and separation from God.

sadness, to old and to young, and to Jew and to Christian. This seems to be because the images of shepherd (verses 1-4) and host (verses. 5,6) are so necessary in every circumstance of life. Whether I am marrying, or burying, whether I am celebrating the joy of birth or grieving the departure of a dear friend, I am glad to do so in the company of the Heavenly Shepherd and the ever-loving Host. The words of the psalm seem mysteriously equally applicable to a banqueting table, to a sacramental occasion, to a family celebration, to a sick room and eventually to a bedside sharing the grief of loss in death.

Psalm 121 *I lift up my eyes to the hills*

The third of this trio of short psalms also addresses personal need. Unlike the two preceding songs, death and Sheol are not named but for the grieving soul there is great reassurance in these widely known lines. The parallels to Psalms 23 are striking.

Psalm 23   the Lord is my Shepherd
Psalm 121   the Lord is your keeper
Psalm 23   I fear no evil when thou art with me
Psalm 121   the Lord will keep you from all evil
Psalm 23   and I shall dwell in the home of the Lord for ever.
Psalm 121   the Lord will keep your going out and your coming in
                    From this time forth and for evermore

The psalmist speaks of 'evermore' which is not the same as the heaven described by Jesus in the New Testament but, as Christians read the psalm, they will recognise a foretaste of these joys. It has been suggested that Ps 121 was written as a pilgrim's farewell to Jerusalem and the Temple and, if this is so, it adds further significance to the psalm as appropriate funeral praise, not only appropriate but hugely comforting. Although none of us knows what language is spoken in heaven I am sure that the psalms will be sung!

Less dramatically, the psalms are already sung, recited, read and preached at almost every Christian believer's funeral. And all this in spite of the fact that there is little or no evidence of an explicit belief in personal immortality in the psalms (or indeed in any part of the Old Testament). When Christians use the psalms, however, they bring to them an added dimension of understanding.

51

Psalms 84 and 90

These two psalms are about living with God. Psalm 84 is about living in God's place and Psalm 90 about living in God's time. They both begin with reference to God's dwelling place and they both develop wonderful word pictures of living together with God. Psalm 84 begins "How lovely is thy dwelling place" and Psalm 90 begins "You have been our dwelling place." A Christian easily transposes these psalms to their own circumstances and recognises that the time and the place both refer to the here and now and to the world beyond.

Ps 84 *At home with God*

Here is concrete imagery to help grieving people feel comfortable. Psalm 84 contains ten synonyms for 'house'. Grieving families who feel uncertain, confused and lost are comforted with pictures of home. When people suffer loss, and do not know which way they should go, here is mention of shepherds who look after lost sheep and hosts who feed hungry travellers, and many images that transcend both place and time. Psalm 90 has as many references to time as Psalm 84 has to dwelling places and they link together the broad sweep of God's view of time and the more limited view of a human life that rarely lasts more than a hundred years When the order of life has been disturbed and chaos threatens, the psalmists are masters of consolation. They speak to their readers and listeners with words that make good sense.

Ps 90. *Lord you have been our dwelling place throughout all generations*

This psalm has been categorised as a 'lament' and, although there is sadness and some disillusionment in the verses, there is also huge comfort. There is pain and joy, there is anguish and ecstasy; there are thunder clouds and blue skies. It is an enigmatic psalm, and human life is enigmatic! Tomorrow remains a mystery, yesterday flies forgotten with the advent of a new day. The psalm reflects upon the course of life with realism and almost a detached indifference. It is both prayer and praise, and the congregation who hears or sings these words with belief will be both chastened and heartened. The psalmist who wrote Ps 90 was not a young man, nor was he a saint, but surely he knew his need and was faithful to his God.

Psalm 103 *Bless the Lord, O my soul; and all that is within me, bless his holy name!*

Here is perfect praise following the end of the earthly life of a good disciple. Here are the thoughts and words to mark the beginning of that believer's fuller, higher life in God's nearer presence. This song seems to be a duet of earthly and heavenly praise. In these thoughts, there is a mystic harmony between the here and the hereafter.

This wonderful psalm of praise sets forth one of the most comprehensive declarations of the love of God found anywhere in the Old Testament. The *love* is that of:

A parent	*-as a Father pities his children*
A forgiving Lord	*-who forgives all your iniquity*
A beneficent benefactor	*-who satisfies you with good things as long as you live*
A healing physician	*- who heals all your diseases*
A redeemer	*- who redeems your life from the pit*
A creator	*-his kingdom rules over all*

Such a caring God pours out his unconditional love upon undeserving humanity.

When Christians hear psalms on funeral occasions, God's word meets human need and they are reassured about the reality of heaven and about the saving power of God. They come away knowing in their hearts that the one they mourn is safe in the everlasting arms. These psalms in particular have the capacity to bridge the gaps of time and place between earth and heaven. All six of these psalms, and many others, allow the worshipper to move easily from here to eternity on behalf of the one they mourn. Sadly, for many people death has come to mean defeat and is the thing most of all to be feared. There is opportunity for Christians every time they share together in funeral worship to tell the world that there is a Hope beyond the sadness of this world which is ours through Jesus Christ. In Christ, the grave is but the entrance to the fuller, nearer presence of God.

WEDDINGS

There are many psalms that have been sung at weddings, perhaps they all have! And that is how it should be. However, five psalms are selected and the reasons for these choices are set out. The five are 23, 67, 103, 127, and 128.

Ps 23 *The Lord is my shepherd*

This is the psalm that not only fits any situation but it is also, as noted above, the overwhelming choice by millions of people for funerals and for weddings. It is personal and it is corporate, it encompasses past, present and future and, probably most importantly in an age of mass disbelief, it is still the psalm that is most widely known and hugely loved. So, it is a wedding choice as well as a funeral choice and there is nothing strange or wrong about that because the words and the accompanying associations allow a huge spectrum of worshippers from a great variety of faith backgrounds to come together for a real worship experience.

Ps 67 *May God be gracious to us and bless us and make his face shine upon us*

These are words and sentiments that those who gather for a wedding may have on their minds. They will be thinking of the bride and the bridegroom and will also be thinking about every other married couple present, and also about those who are no longer married, and they will not be forgetting those who have never been married. This is a good frame of mind and heart to approach the prayers and the vows that are to be said in the service. Here is a psalm that invites praise from all *"May all the people praise you O God."* And in as far as Christians interpret what they sing, albeit unconsciously, they will sing the psalms through the mediation of Jesus Christ. This is not easily expressed or grasped and yet many of the saints of previous generations have shared this realisation that all those who call Christ 'Lord' are prepared *to* attempt to live their lives and give meaning to their lives through Jesus Christ. The psalms were an integral part of the life of Jesus, in his praying, his teaching and his relationship to God his Father and will be the same for all follow Him, albeit to a lesser degree.

Ps 103 *Praise the Lord O my soul*

Like Ps 23, this is often chosen for both funerals and weddings. This great hymn expresses the psalmist's gratitude to God and his dependence upon God. These are appropriate words and sentiments for any couple marrying and for their family and friends. Ps 103 also majors on forgiveness and forgiveness has to be a part of any good marriage. Any number of the individual verses could be selected as an appropriate mantra for a wedding day, or for a good life e.g. Praise the Lord O my soul and forget not all his benefits.

Ps 127,128 *Except the Lord build the house…. Blessed is everyone who fears the Lord….*

Psalms 127 and 128 are both short and contain many wise words for those intending to marry. Perhaps these psalms are most appropriate for young couples as both psalms breathe a spirit of almost unqualified optimism and confidence. It is the first line of Ps 127 that is probably most defining and all else follows from that line. In the opinion of many, these psalms were originally composed for pilgrims going up to Jerusalem for the great annual festivals like Atonement, Ingathering and Passover. The parallel between pilgrimage and marriage is a very good one and, for those who accept the implications, these two psalms are a good foundation for both life and marriage.

DISCUSSION TOPICS

1. What makes particular psalms and hymns appropriate for weddings and for funerals?

2. How is it that Ps 23 is appropriate for a funeral service and for a marriage ceremony?

CHAPTER FIVE

PSALMS AND THE NEW TESTAMENT

Psalms is the most quoted Old Testament book in the New Testament. At least sixty of the one hundred and fifty psalms are quoted in seventeen New Testament books, and the total number of quotations is about one hundred and fifty-five. There are also some other New Testament texts where a psalm may be alluded to. Approximately seventy of these quotations are in the Gospels and of these approximately twenty-five are instances where Jesus' reported speech is quoted from the psalms. The authors in both the Old and New Testaments show themselves to be very familiar with the psalms, quoting either the exact words as we have them or words very close to the words we know.

In an age when there was no printing and the production of books was by manual copying clearly more was demanded of memory and certainly the New Testament authors knew and quoted easily from the psalms that they knew so well. Sometimes the way psalms are used in the New Testament is different from contemporary use and it can be disturbing to find interpretations very different from familiar interpretations. They are used in ways that we do not immediately understand, and some of the psalms which are quoted are not particularly well known nowadays. With one exception, it is not likely that any of the six most quoted psalms in the New Testament will be included in contemporary lists of popular psalms. The six psalms most quoted are Psalms 2, 8, 22, 69, 110 and 118. From this list only Psalm 8 would be termed a popular psalm today. Psalm 110 is the most quoted of all: of the twenty-one times, it is quoted in the New Testament, seven are in the Gospels and all are attributed to Jesus.

The majority of these most quoted psalms are recognised by both Jews and Christians as strongly messianic (i.e. foretelling the coming of a messiah) and even those which are not have messianic tendencies. Not only were they interpreted messianically by the New Testament authors but they are still, in the main, interpreted in this way by many Christians.

The six most quoted psalms when categorised by modern psalm type classification comprise two Individual Laments (22,69), two Royal

Psalms (2,110), one Individual Song of Thanksgiving (118) and one Hymn (8).[14]

Psalm 110: *The Messiah and Melchizedek the priest*

The Lord says to my Lord:
"Sit at my right hand, till I make your enemies your footstool."
The Lord sends forth from Zion your mighty sceptre.
Rule in the midst of your foes!
Your people will offer themselves freely
on the day you lead your host upon the holy mountains.
From the womb of the morning like dew your youth will come to you.
The Lord has sworn and will not change his mind,
"You are a priest forever after the order of Melchizedek."
The Lord is at your right hand;
he will shatter kings on the day of his wrath.
He will execute judgment among the nations, filling them with corpses;
he will shatter chiefs over the wide earth.
He will drink from the brook by the way; therefore, he will lift up his head.

Psalm 110.1 *"The Lord says to my Lord, 'Sit at my right hand until I make your enemies a footstool for your feet"* is quoted in whole or in part, 15 times, making it the Old Testament's most quoted *verse* in the New Testament and, of these quotations, 6 are spoken by Jesus. In addition, verse 4 is quoted five times making this psalm also the most quoted in the New Testament. Of all the psalms which are given the designation 'messianic' this seems to be the one, along with Psalm 2, which is deemed most messianic by the early Church.

Modern interpretation of this psalm has recognised many difficulties and it is not surprising that a large number of widely differing suggestions have been put forward. It would seem most likely that the speaker is a Temple servant, perhaps a prophet or a priest, addressing the king. If that assumption is made, the psalm can be understood to be addressed to King David or to one of his successors. This is the way the

---

[14] Bernard Anderson (1983), *Out of the Depths,* Philadelphia: Westminster, pp. 235ff.

verse seems to have been understood by Jesus and others in the New Testament. Jesus interpreted it messianically as a reference to himself and to this day this is how the psalm has often been interpreted.

If David himself is the speaker, the identity of 'David's Lord' as understood by David is much more difficult to understand. Whereas we, with hindsight, can identify David's Lord, we have to wonder how David understood the identity of 'his lord', whereas if the psalm be addressed *to* David by a priest, the psalm's interpretation becomes easier.

We can thus associate the psalm with David or one of his line, perhaps even written by David, but written as a psalm to be addressed to a king by a prophet or a priest. Verse 4 speaking of the ancient priest/king Melchizedek is a reference to Genesis 14.18ff. The implication for modern interpreters is to remind us that Christ is a priest as well as a king.

In spite of these difficulties Psalm 110 was very significant in the New Testament and remained so throughout the Christian centuries.

Psalm 2: *What do the nations conspire?*

This psalm and Psalm 118 are among 34 'orphan' psalms that are psalms without superscriptions. From the time of Jesus until the completion of the New Testament, Rome ruled in Judea. The Zealots and many other Jews longed for Israel to be an independent sovereign state and a psalm such as this will have expressed the national longing to have a Davidic king back on the throne. Psalm 2 will have been heard messianically where the messiah the people wanted will have been a human deliverer who would free the people from the oppression they were suffering under the Roman authorities. When the Church took over the Old Testament and began to interpret the psalms they will have understood Jesus as having already fulfilled Psalm 2. For them the references to David as a type of the One to Come will have been to Christ, as an all-conquering Messiah.

Ps 2 is thus a highly political psalm teaching us how to pray political prayers and reminding us that, not only is our Heavenly Father concerned about our individual needs, petitions and desires, but also about the whole created realm. Even the politics and laws of the nations are under his scrutiny. God cares about the big stage as well as the little one.

It has been suggested by Peterson (1987) that many believers are comfortable and are able to bring their individual prayers before God, but they are less confident that God can also be trusted to manage the political affairs of nations!

Undoubtedly this psalm will have been sung with great fervour and will have been a favourite with the more nationalistically minded of the disciples of Jesus such as Peter, John and Simon the Zealot. Jesus never quoted this psalm himself but the most famous use of the psalm was following the baptism of Jesus by John the Baptist, when a voice from heaven was heard to say:

This is my beloved Son, with whom I am well pleased. (Mt. 3.17)

Although only Matthew and Mark record John as baptising Jesus, the other Gospels also quote this psalm though in slightly different contexts; compare Mark 1.11; Luke 3.22; and John 1.49. This psalm is quoted at least 10 times in the New Testament.

Psalm 8: *O Lord, our Lord, how majestic is thy name in all the earth*

This psalm, like Psalms 22, 69 and 110, is designated a psalm of David in the superscription preceding the psalm. As previously noted these superscriptions, although not parts of the original psalms, are nevertheless of great antiquity. They are reproduced in the Hebrew Masoretic Text, and in almost all translations since then, but it is necessary to remember that they are not as old as the psalms to which they are attached.

Psalm 8 can be classified as a hymn of praise to God. There is extensive use of royal language and in that way Psalm 8 may also be considered to be a messianic psalm.

Yet thou hast made him little less than God,
and dost crown him with glory and honour.
Thou hast given him dominion over the works of thy hands.

This can be understood to refer to humanity in general or can also refer to One particular human being who will be Messiah.

At a time when Israel was suffering the indignity of being occupied and ruled by Rome, such words would have been sweet music to the ears of all loyal Jews, loyal that is to the faith of their fore fathers. Here their faith in the sovereignty and might of God is reaffirmed and they are again able to stand up straight and feel proud of their history, and realize their destiny. This short psalm is also a beautiful hymn of creation and, perhaps most significantly of all, the psalm bears testimony to the very special place that human beings have in the sight of God. This alone has rendered the psalm popular and important at any time and in any place when people feel insecure and threatened. Psalm 8 is still very popular and much loved today, although the reasons may be a little different.

This psalm acknowledges man's high status and it can also be understood Messianically because all God's people are looking forward to the realisation of the rule of God and this will only come to pass when Messiah returns.

Psalm 22: *My God, my God, why hast thou forsaken me?*

This is an individual lament and was immortalised when Jesus quoted from verse 1 as he hung upon the Cross of Calvary. "*My God, my God, why hast thou forsaken me?*" Very much has been written about Jesus' use of this verse. What did He really mean? Did He think that God his Heavenly Father had abandoned Him?

By using these words Jesus identified to the fullest extent possible with the desolation of anyone and everyone who has ever felt out of contact with the living God. By so doing, and by quoting this psalm which soon progresses to a positive affirmation from verse 19 onwards, Jesus has led despairing believers back to the throne of grace. This psalm also illustrates how very few psalms conform exclusively to one type. Psalm 22 begins as an Individual Lament but comes around in the final verses to use the language of praise and proclamation.

Like Psalms 2 and 110, Psalm 22 is a classic messianic psalm. Here the psalmist recounts how Israel trusted God and was not disappointed. The psalm is addressed to God Himself and for Jews the psalm expresses the same messianic confidence that God will restore Israel's fortunes:

Posterity shall serve him;
Men shall tell of the Lord to the coming generation,
and proclaim his deliverance to a people yet unborn,
that he has wrought it. (Ps. 22.30-31)

Christians have also interpreted it messianically seeing the psalm as a prediction of the Second Coming of Christ and understanding the references to Christ's final victories.

Psalm 69: *Save me O God, for the waters have come up to my neck*

This lament is not easy to read or straightforward to understand for not only is it a lament, it is also one of the cursing psalms where the psalmist calls upon God to vindicate him against his enemies and asks that they receive awful punishments.

The cursing psalms are also difficult for us to pray for we know that, while we may feel such sentiments, we also know that we ought not to say them and certainly not to pray them! Here we find the Psalter being most painfully honest. This is how human beings behave! In complete contrast, there is the wonderfully humble verse 6.

> Let not those who hope in thee be put to shame through me,
> O Lord God of hosts;
> let not those who seek thee be brought to dishonour through me.

This suggests the prayer *"O Lord let not my thoughts, words or deeds, turn anyone away from you"*.

However, this is also a strongly Messianic psalm which looks forward to the universal reign of God and of His Son Jesus Christ. It may well be that its strongly messianic character made it a more popular psalm in the First Century than nowadays. There was then a greater expectation of the end of the world.

The psalm is quoted fifteen times in the New Testament, with seven of its thirty-six verses being quoted. Clearly it was very well known in the early Church. Jesus is reported as quoting from verses 4 and 21: *"More in number than the hairs of my head are those who hate me without cause; mighty are those who would destroy me, those who attack me with lies. What I did not steal must I now restore?"* (v. 4) quoted in John 15.25 *"They hated me without a cause"* and *"They gave me poison for food, and for my thirst they gave me vinegar to drink"* (v. 21) quoted in John 19.29 *"a bowl full of vinegar stood there"*.

A cursing psalm like this one, which expresses unchristian sentiments, worries many people. How can Christians read or say such things and what place have such things in the Word of God? Many people have written about this problem. C.S. Lewis' Reflections on the

Psalms published in 1958 has helped many generations to a better understanding (in Chapter 6 there is a fuller discussion of these cursing psalms).

Psalm 118: *O give thanks to the Lord for he is good, his steadfast love endures forever.*

This psalm may be classified as an individual song of thanksgiving, but this is not the only sound coming from the psalm for we also hear a congregation at praise, and we can identify two proverbial sayings in verses 8 and 9 which are Wisdom literature, as well as a strong liturgical emphasis. This psalm was a Passover song, and so reverberates with all the excitement of that great occasion.

For Christians the verses 22, 23, 25, 26 are very familiar because there are quotations from these verses in the traditional readings for Palm Sunday and for Holy Week. This indicates to us that for a very long time Christians have interpreted this psalm messianically.

> The stone which the builders rejected
> has become the head of the corner.
> This is the Lord's doing,
> is marvellous in our eyes.
> Save us, we beseech thee, O Lord!
> O Lord, we beseech thee, give us success!
> Blessed be he who enters in the name of the Lord!
> We bless you from the house of the Lord.

OTHER USES OF PSALMS IN THE NEW TESTAMENT

Psalms are quoted in many books of the New Testament. This is further evidence of the dependence of the New Testament upon the Old. Although the whole Gospel is not contained in the Old Testament, the whole Gospel cannot be preached without reference to the Old Testament. In order to understand many of the leading ideas in the New Testament it is necessary to turn to the Old Testament and that is in fact how the psalms are used in the New Testament both on the lips of Jesus and in other parts of the narrative.

THE PSALMS, AND THE LORD'S PRAYER

The disciples ask Jesus to teach them how to pray. He produced no new theory of prayer, other than to take the elements of prayer as they are present in the Old Testament and present them to the disciples, freed from traditional liturgical shape and ritual form *"Our Father who art in heaven, hallowed be thy Name"* is a re-statement of phrases such as:

But the Lord sits enthroned for ever, he has established his throne for judgment;
and he judges the world with righteousness, he judges the people with equity. (Ps. 9.7-8) and
Those who trust in the Lord are like Mount Zion,
which cannot be moved, but abides for ever. (Ps. 125.1)
"How lovely is thy dwelling place, O Lord of hosts to me!" (Ps 84.1)

Other texts expressing the same elements as the first phrase include: Ps 11.4; 14.2; 29.10; 46.4-7; 33.1; 33.7. The second phrase, *"Thy kingdom come, Thy will be done on earth as it is in heaven"* is a paraphrasing of lines like:

O sing to the Lord a new song,
for he has done marvellous things! (Ps. 98.1)
Clap your hands, all peoples!
Shout to God with loud songs of joy!
For the Lord, the Most High, is terrible,
A great king over all the earth.
He subdued peoples under us,
and nations under our feet.
He chose our heritage for you,
the pride of Jacob whom he loves. (Ps. 47.1-4)
And other quotations such as Ps. 57.11; 67.5-7; 126.1.

In similar manner, we can go right through the Lord's Prayer, phrase by phrase, and find verses from the psalms which are prayers, and which effectively express the same messages as the six petitions of the Lord's prayer - with one exception. The exception seems to be the second half of the fourth petition. The fourth petition is *"Forgive us our trespasses as we forgive those who trespass against us"*, or the alternative form, *"Forgive us our debts as we forgive our debtors"* (or the more contemporary *"Forgive us our sins... "*).

It is the second part of this fourth petition for which there are no obvious precedents in the Psalter. There is the Deuteronomy passage (15.1ff) on the relief of debt at the end of seven years, and the Jubilee passages in Leviticus (25.1ff) which do enshrine the essence of the need to forgive debt. We are however made plainly aware in the Gospels and other books of the New Testament of the necessity for us to forgive others if we ourselves want to be forgiven. We may also note in passing that psychologically speaking it is only possible to accept forgiveness when we ourselves have given forgiveness to another or to others.

One further aspect of the psalms is worthy of mention. How many messianic psalms are there? This is a part of the bigger question; How much of the Old Testament can be read messianically by Christians? The answer of course seems to be that there are a great number of passages, including a large number of psalms, to which Christians may attach messianic interpretations. While there will never be complete agreement, there does seem to be a growing awareness that there are very many texts to which Christians may attach Messianic interpretations. Indeed, the Christian community has "baptised the Psalter into Christ".[15]

The fact that Jesus identified himself as the Messiah on several recorded occasions is a further compelling reason for the Christian community to read the Psalter and the Old Testament messianically. This means that we need to read the Old Testament in two ways: reading it first as it was originally, the scriptures of the Jews, but then we need to read it a second time as Christians looking for fulfilment, wherever we may find it. It is also important to note that psalms about a messianic king are only one way to identify the Messiah in the Old Testament, whereas the other is as the One who suffers and this Messiah is portrayed in the psalms, particularly Psalms 22 and 40.

The foregoing are a range of examples of psalm passages which enhance and clarify our concept of the Messiah, the One who was to come, and whom we know has come as our Saviour Jesus Christ, and who we know will come again, in glory.

---

[15] Bernard Anderson, (1983), *Out of the Depths,* Philadelphia: Westminster, pp. 15ff, referring to W.T. Davidson.

DISCUSSION TOPIC

The Book of Psalms can be compared to a bridge which links the Old and New Testaments.   Discuss this image and find your own illustrations.

CHAPTER SIX

SOME DIFFICULT PSALMS

There are two groups of psalms that many people find difficult to read and for completely different reasons: the imprecatory psalms and those in which the psalmist makes extravagant claims for his virtue.

The first group, the imprecatory psalms, curse enemies within and enemies without, curse God's enemies and the psalmist's enemies. They deride the wicked and even criticise God himself. These have always been difficult for Christians to read because undisguised hatred seems an affront to a God of love, and is plainly not a Christian response to anybody. It may well be an appropriate response to sin but not to the sinner.

In these psalms, the psalmist often calls upon God to kill the evil doers, to wound them, to leave them without progeny, and to embarrass and oppress them in a hundred different ways. Nothing seems to be too bad a treatment to have meted out to these enemies of the psalmist whom he assumes are also the enemies of God. Even that most beautiful psalm, the Twenty Third, expresses a selfish and unloving sentiment towards his enemies who were presumably hungry, and who had to watch when the psalmist recounts how God had prepared and set out a feast for him!

You prepare a table before me,
In the presence of my enemies
You anoint my head with oil
My cup overflows. (Ps 23.5)

There are at least twenty of these cursing psalms. They include Ps9, Ps 21, Ps 23, Ps 69, 119, verses 17-24, Ps 120, and Ps 137. The assumption is made that God and Israel are totally and mutually involved with each other, and the psalmist is quite prepared to ask God to do any number of evil things to his enemies and to anyone else whom the psalmist judges wicked! These psalms are difficult for both Jews and Christians to read with any degree of acceptance and comfort. How are they to be read?

Whereas children express hatred, grown up people do not easily do so, if for no better reason that it would almost certainly bring recriminations upon themselves. They would end up suffering a great deal more than those upon whom they were foolish enough to vent their anger. These psalms want God to take revenge upon the psalmist's enemies and, in so far as the reader of the psalms in almost every case is urged or by implication is urged to identify with the psalmist, readers find themselves asking God to take revenge upon enemies. This is certainly not a Christian response to adversaries.

Why then are these sentiments expressed in the psalms? The following appear to be some of the reasons:

1. This is humanity like it really is! While hatred may be hidden, disguised, sublimated or denied it is nevertheless present in every age and culture. It seems that people of the Ancient Near East were more open about expressing hatred and were much more practised in issuing curses than at least some in the first years of our twenty first century. Children today openly express hatred especially in moments of frustration or annoyance when denied what they want by their parents; mature adults are expected to have a tighter control of their emotions.

2. The presence of these psalms in the Psalter demonstrates how seriously Israel took sin. There is no doubt that all the moral leaders in ancient Israel considered that Yahweh, the righteous God, was a moral God, who abhorred sin in any form. Thus, the God of Israel and the people of Israel seemed to take sin more seriously than any of the nations in neighbouring countries. Ps 31.6 expresses well the psalmist's conviction of how much God, and therefore his special people, hate sin, "*I hate those who cling to worthless idols, I trust in the Lord*".

3. Psalm readers are therefore encouraged to identify with this deep hatred of sin in order to abhor the sin if not the sinner. It seems that Israel made less distinction between the sin and the sinner than Jesus did in his ministry. The positive side of this is that all who read the psalms are warned not even to connive with sin. There is an ancient Chinese proverb "*Never stoop when walking through a cucumber patch!*", that is, do not even give any grounds for suspicion.

4. The presence of God in the cursing psalms is also an invitation to

bring everything to God in prayer. God is a loving Heavenly Parent who wants his children to share all their concerns with Him. God loves his children with an everlasting and complete love. Eugene Peterson (1987), who wrote *Psalms, Prayers of the Heart*, entitled one chapter 'Praying our hate!' and he cites Ps 137, which is a model of compassion and concern until its final three verses:

"Remember, O Lord what the Edomites did on the day Jerusalem fell
'Tear it down' they cried, 'tear it down to its foundations'.
Daughter of Babylon, doomed to destruction, happy is he who repays you for what you have done to us, he who seizes your infants and dashes them against the rocks "

It is less difficult to bring fears and hopes, as well as needs and petitions to God but Eugene Peterson (1987) is correct when he also urges worshippers to bring their hate, lust and greed, their selfishness and inattention, their intimidation and doubt as well as praise, adoration and all the respectable things to God in prayer.

Nevertheless, it is difficult and indeed no one has any moral right to urge such hatred upon God and in fact almost to dictate to God what punishment he should mete out on those "wicked" ones, when we are all too aware that we ourselves often exhibit all the characteristics of fallen humanity. They are a necessary although unwelcome part of the canon of Holy Scripture.

All believers need to wrestle and pray about these psalms. In summarising it is necessary to recognise that Israel was a much persecuted nation and may at times have had a persecution complex. There was in Israel a passion to distinguish good from evil, and this was one of the marks that made Israel so different from many of her neighbours. These psalms recognise the darker side of humanity and this is how all people are for part of the time. These psalms pray for the defeat of evil, and are aware of the danger of associating with both evil people and evil things.

Positively these cursings continually remind their readers that there is a battle to be fought, and all who are in Christ know that it was only Jesus who was able to rout the enemy when He engaged all things evil on the Cross and emerged victorious from the grave. His victory and the necessary armour and weapons to engage all the powers of evil are recorded in Ephesians 6.10-20

The second group of difficult psalms are those in which the psalmist makes extravagant claims for his virtue, his righteousness and his obedience to all the many parts of the Law of God. In several of these there seems to be almost a spirit of self-righteousness, of the kind that Jesus was later to condemn in the Pharisees.

A phrase like Ps 119.53 at one and the same time is both a curse against the wicked, and a statement of self-praise. *"Indignation grips me because of the wicked, who have forsaken your law"*. It is a brave person who proclaims publicly *"The law of thy mouth is better to me than thousands of gold and silver pieces."* Yes indeed, a true word, but if believers receive the spirit of Psalm 131 would they ever say such things? Again, it is either a brave or a foolish person who claims with the words of Ps 119.93 *"I will never forget your precepts for by them you have preserved my life"*.

Ps 26 seems to be one of the most explicit statement of this pharisaic-like hypocrisy and is very difficult to reconcile with the touching humility and realism of Ps 131 which Jesus was later to exemplify. Such lines as *"I have trusted in the Lord without wavering"* and *"I wash my hands in innocence and go about thy altar, O Lord, singing aloud a song of thanksgiving"*.

Psalm 1 also breathes a spirit of perfection that is not a characteristic of human nature.

For slightly different reasons some of the Royal Psalms such as Ps 2 and Ps 110 are also difficult to engage with, for the very reason of their *messianic outlook.* These psalms appear to be directly addressed to God's anointed one and as such today's readers, or readers in any age, can only overhear such words as not primarily intended for our ear or indeed even for those of the psalmist. In addition, Ps 22, which has been immortalised for Christians by Jesus quoting its opening words from the Cross, is for the same reason difficult to engage with because Jesus using these words has, in the minds of Christians, made this his own psalm rather than that of subsequent generations of believers, and further when verses 8 and 18 are also quoted in the Gospels this particular interpretation is intensified.

Can contemporary readers identify with,

"My God, my God why has thou forsaken me?"

How then can these psalms be understood? Is it possible that those psalms which cannot be received or used personally, can only be heard, read and spoken as it were by Jesus Himself? Those psalms that no human being can make their own and the hopes and fears, the praises and confessions, the laments and thanksgivings can in fact only be spoken and only be accepted by Jesus Himself. This allows the believer insofar as he is one with his Lord, to hear and speak these psalms only as Jesus hears and speaks them.

Expressed simply, only Jesus alone is good enough to curse wickedness for what it is, and only Jesus himself is good enough to merit the titles and accolades which no mere human can ever merit or deserve. And finally, only Jesus can receive the highly charged messianic hymns as he fulfils them in himself. So, all that believers can do with such verses in such psalms is to hear Jesus say them, as they are invited to sit at His feet.

Because His life on earth was perfect He can say of the wicked to God, His Father *"They gave me poison for food, and for my thirst they gave me vinegar to drink."* And God by His mercy has become incarnate in His Son so that the wicked may repent and be led back to grace. The model of the elder brother's reception back into the arms of his father has been wonderfully captured by Rembrandt's painting of The Return of Prodigal Son (which hangs in the Hermitage Gallery in St Petersburg).

DISCUSSION TOPIC

How does the New Testament use these difficult psalms?

CHAPTER SEVEN

CLASSIFYING PSALMS

In Chapter 8, each psalm will be studied in two ways. In the first, answers will be offered to 9 questions about the psalm in table form. The information contained in the tables carries no particular authority, nor does it make any claim to be original. The information gathered is simply a summary of much that has been written over many years. In the second part of each page the **message and the meaning** of the psalm is explored in two or three short paragraphs.

Psalm Number and Title.

These titles have been gathered from a variety of sources. The choices are somewhat arbitrary and many others are possible. Nevertheless, a title helps to identify a psalm and the challenge remains with the reader to choose or affirm a chosen title that is significant. The only Bible version not including Psalm titles is the New English Bible. All the other versions append either the original or another title.

Book, Number of verses and a Key Verse or verses

Book	
Number of verses	
Key verse	

Book refers to the collection of all the psalms into five 'books'. It is also helpful to identify each psalm with the particular book in which it is to be found **(Books I, II, III, IV or V)**. These 'Books' refer to five collections that were made before the whole Psalter was assembled in probably the third century BC. This is the first question of the smaller table, followed by the number of verses and a key verse. The **Number of verses** is clearly a fixed number and is given by the verse number except in the psalms which conclude a given 'Book' and in those five instances there will be doxologies added to the text to bring each 'book' to a close. The whole collection is concluded with Ps 150 which is in fact an extended doxology for the completed collection. The number of verses varies enormously, 3 psalms have only 3 verses each (Psalms 131,133,134) while the longest (Ps 119) has 176; the second longest (Ps 78) has 72 verses.

As with a title, a **key verse** is a matter of individual choice and it's the verse that seems to make the greatest impact on the reader, and allows the reader to personalise their choice.

Main table

Type of psalm	
Possible original usage and setting	
Including prayer or not	
Individual or Communal	
Date and author	
Subsequent and Contemporary significance - Messianic indications	

The **Psalm Type** has been briefly discussed in Chapter Two. Over the past 150 years many classifications have been suggested. No two lists are in complete agreement. The scholars who have advanced these ideas have all made a contribution to the total knowledge of psalm classification and it seems that each subsequent scheme offers a refinement on what went before. For the purposes of this book, the simplest of schemes has been chosen and four types of psalm are identified. This follows closely on the work of W.H. Bellinger (2012), and his scholarship and contribution are gratefully acknowledged.

The four types are **Lament** (about 65), **Praise** (about 60), **Wisdom** (about 11), and **Royal** (also about 11), making a total of about 147. It is necessary to justify the term 'about'. There are two reasons for this qualification: the first is that many psalms show the marks of more than one type, and the second reason is that no two definitions of any given type are quite the same. As a psalm is read it is challenging to practice 'Type Identification' and at times very frustrating! The **Lament psalms** express contrition, disappointment, anger, sadness but often items for praise and thanksgiving will be included. Similarly, the **Praise psalms** will be mainly positive and upbeat but may include less than happy statements. Thus, from time to time, many commentators on the psalms will differ in their assessment of a psalm and at other times speak of a mixed type psalm showing signs of more than one type. There are two groups of psalms majoring on Royalty, one group designate God as King, and the other designate a man of God's choosing as king. Following Bellinger (2012) and others it is this latter description that identifies 11 **Royal** Psalms for the purposes of this book. The **Wisdom** psalms are probably the best defined group, but even with this category there are other psalms which include some 'wise' teaching and vocabulary but are thought to be less than definitively 'wise'. (It is in the Book of Proverbs that Wisdom is most clearly set out).

The **Possible original usage and setting** is a clumsy phrase encouraging the reader to try to imagine where the psalm would most probably have first been used and whether it would have been sung or recited or used in some other way. The majority seem to have been written for use in worship, often in the Temple at Jerusalem. However, there are some psalms which are much more personal, and still others which seem to have been written more for purposes of instruction. There are also a number which appear to have been written for particular occasions, an annual religious festival, or the celebration of the Enthronement of God as monarch.

The question about prayer is much more straightforward. The context allows the reader to decide whether or not the psalm is a prayer, or is in part a prayer, or is not a prayer at all. This is an important question because it allows the reader to better understand the writer's intentions.

Many psalms are addressed to **a congregation**, or express the mind of a congregation. Other psalms are clearly spoken by **an individual** on his own account in either prayer or praise or meditation. The question about **singular or plural** is useful in order to more fully appreciate the context. However, a significant number of psalms move from singular to plural or plural to singular, and some do so more than once.

The matter of **date and authorship** has already been mentioned. These questions which are related are among the most difficult to decide. Scholars often vary hugely in their assessments of the date; very often there is little agreement and seldom is there anything like an exact date offered. With the earliest pre-exilic psalms, there is the greatest likelihood of Davidic authorship. Even then many authorities prefer to attribute an early psalm to 'King David or a Davidic king'. For the other types of origin, usually the most exact identification is to a 'Temple official', to 'a cult priest' to a 'prophet' or perhaps to a 'wise man'.

The final question about **subsequent or contemporary significance and messianic indications** is, like several other questions, a matter of individual decision. The crucial importance of the question is that the reader is able to ponder the impact of the psalm at the time of writing, and later, and at any point in the Church's subsequent history. And in particular the reader will begin to identify the psalms that were influential at the time the New Testament was being written and those used most frequently by the Church up to and including the present time. However, many psalms will find more than one use and probably Ps 23 is the outstanding example of a psalm that is appropriate and powerful in both individual and plural settings and in many different situations.

In the second 'message and meaning' part of the page, little more is attempted than to point the reader towards possible lines of enquiry, and to attempt sometimes to identify some of the unique features that may have characterised a particular psalm.

DISCUSSION TOPICS

1. Suggest further questions which could be asked of any psalm.
2. Either write a short psalm or re-write a biblical psalm in contemporary English.

CHAPTER EIGHT

THE MEANING AND THE MESSAGE OF EACH PSALM

Psalm 1. Doing things God's way.

Book	I
Number of verses	6
Key verse	3

Type of psalm	Wisdom
Possible original usage and setting	Probably a reflective psalm for personal use
Including prayer or not	Not a prayer as such
Individual or Communal	Individual
Date and author	Post exilic, author unknown
Subsequent and Contemporary significance - Messianic indications	In any age Christians as well as Jews can reflect upon life in these words.

Psalm 1 expresses the orthodox belief at the time it was written – God blesses obedience and punishes disobedience.

This is the first of the 11 Wisdom psalms in the Psalter (1, 32, 37, 49, 73, 78, 112, 119, 127, 128 and 133). Psalm 1 is also a preface to the whole Psalter. It sets out the rules for good living, and it both echoes some of the Ten Commandments; it is also reminiscent of the Book of Job and of Proverbs 3.1-6. Some would see this psalm as more appropriate for private reflection than for public or liturgical worship. Indeed, it seems more appropriate for a classroom than a pulpit. Psalm 1 may be compared to the beatitudes and comparable to Matthew 5.1ff.

Psalm 1 is quoted in Jeremiah 17.5-8 and is often sung (e.g. as in the Church Hymnary of the Church of Scotland 4, Hymn 1, "How blest are those who do not stray," paraphrased by Charles Robertson in the twentieth century).

Psalm 2. God's chosen king.

Book	I
Number of verses	12
Key verses	10 & 11

Type of psalm	Royal
Possible original usage and setting	In Temple worship at the Annual Enthronement occasion
Including prayer or not	No, an address to the nations
Individual or Communal	Communal and individual
Date and author	Pre-exilic, by David, a Davidic king or a cultic prophet
Subsequent and Contemporary significance - Messianic indications	For Jew and Christian a highly significant prophetic text – the One to Come. Related in content to Psalm 110

Psalm 2 along with Psalm 1 introduces the whole Psalter. Psalm 2 is the first of the 11 Royal Psalms (along with Psalms 18, 20, 21, 45, 72, 89, 101, 110, 132 and 144). They all focus on God's regent on earth who was originally King David when the psalm was written and his subsequent successors. (including for example Psalm 93 which focus on God himself as King).

The King of Israel has a special place, and a particular role in God's affection and calling them to be the Chosen People. Psalm 2 makes a statement about the supremacy of God's anointed one and it is this statement that accounts for the frequency with which Psalms 2.7 and 2.8-9 are quoted in the New Testament. These New Testament usages of Psalm 2 will in all likelihood have influenced Handel to include these words for the Messiah four times.

Psalm 2 is one of a small number of psalms understood to be explicitly Messianic psalms by both Jews and Christians. The psalm is focussed on God designating power, dominion and authority upon his only begotten Son.

Psalm 3. A strong man in trouble.

Book	I
Number of verses	8
Key verse	3a

Type of psalm	Lament
Possible original usage and setting	Possibly a King's lament before God in the Temple.
Including prayer or not	Prayer
Individual or Communal	Individual
Date and author	Pre-exilic, but vocabulary indicates after David's time.
Subsequent and Contemporary significance - Messianic indications	Whether or not by King David this psalm sets the pattern for the King's obedience.

Psalm 3 is a lament but it is not all doom and gloom! It is the first prayer in the Psalter and the first psalm identified with David in its title. The story of the psalm is a man saying his prayers and reflecting upon them, and resting content in his faith. Here is a model for prayer, and also a refection that will be common to others. This private prayer will have been echoed by countless thousands over hundreds of years. As has been noted it is probably impossible to be dogmatic as to whether King David is, or is not, to be identified with the suppliant of the prayer. There are about 70 psalms identified with David in their heading and the majority opinion would be that it is unlikely that dogmatic answers are possible.

Psalm 3 may be a lament but it is a lament filled with confidence, and the deliverance mentioned (v.7) is that delivered by God.

Psalm 4. God is my refuge, my joy and my safety.

Book	I
Number of verses	8
Key verse	8

Type of psalm	Lament, but not a pure lament
Possible original usage and setting	Sung in the Temple as a penitential psalm
Including prayer or not	Prayer
Individual or Communal	Both individual and communal in use
Date and author	Pre-exilic, but probably after David's time
Subsequent and Contemporary significance - Messianic indications	This is everyman's prayer and as such has had continuing significance through the Jewish and Christian eras.

This psalm seems to have been uttered by both priest and people. The leader spoke both for himself and for the congregation in the Temple setting but the prayer is also valid for the suppliant on his own. Verses 4 and 8 suggest that the psalm is to be used as an evening act of devotion.

The psalm suggests this prayer:

Lord in your Word you and I can talk things over,
This is great!
I know I'm cross too often and often unreasonable.
But when I talk things over with you, God life makes more sense!
When I talk to you, you are close again and I can go peacefully to sleep.
Lord you put me together again.
Amen
(Gordon R 2003 pg.3)

Expressed less formally people are often S.I.G. (selfish, intolerant and greedy), but with God can be T.U.G. (tolerant, unselfish and generous)!

Psalm 5. Help me in the morning Lord.

Book	1
Number of verses	12
Key verse	1&12

Type of psalm	Lament
Possible original usage and setting	At the morning liturgy in the Temple.
Including prayer or not	Prayer – perhaps a king's prayer.
Individual or Communal	An individual prays on behalf of others.
Date and author	Probably post-exilic, author unknown priest or other Temple official.
Subsequent and Contemporary significance - Messianic indications	For a Christian, this is a good psalm to read on a Saturday evening before worship on Sunday, and perhaps this is how Psalm 5 has been read for generations.

Although the title names David, this is not a particularly Davidic psalm for it seems to come from a later date with a more developed style of community worship. Here is a pious soul who desires to draw close to God. This may well be a king's prayer but it is also everyman's prayer as are so many psalms. It is this applicability that has rendered psalms as worship for all for so many hundreds of years.

Here is a psalm of oscillating mood and changing fortunes so typical of the human condition. In Psalm 5 there is up and down, there is good and evil, there is praise and criticism and as the psalmist is pulled one way and the other. His assessment of his enemies' changes so each reader is confronted with their own dilemmas. Here psalmist and reader are in conversation.

Psalm 6. I'm sick, Lord! A plea for healing and justice.

Book	I
Number of verses	10
Key verse	6

Type of psalm	Lament
Possible original usage and setting	Used in cultic worship, as a cry for help.
Including prayer or not	Prayer, at least in v. 1-6, but perhaps not v 8-10
Individual or Communal	Individual
Date and author	Although the superscription indicates David other evidence is lacking
Subsequent and Contemporary significance - Messianic indications	Psalm 6 will have been everyman's cry for help. This will explain Psalm 6 as one of the Penitential psalms.

Christians have designated seven psalms as penitential psalms: 6, 32, 38, 51, 102,130 and 143. The most well-known of these is Psalm 51, however all seven are classic repentance texts. These are the psalms "that give words to pray for those who can hardly find any" (pg. 60-61D Kidner 1973). Removed as we are in time and place from the original context it is difficult, if not impossible, to tell the nature of the suppliant's tears and fears.

Verse 5 represents the classic Old Testament view of death, which is that after death there is little expectation of any further existence. Although there are some very few isolated texts which some say suggest otherwise, the majority opinion and the great contrast to the New Testament is that in the Old Testament view, life ends with death, whereas the New Testament teaches that beyond the grave there is a fuller, better life for all who are in Christ.

Verses 8-10 seem to represent a change of subject and a different enemy. It may either be the same psalmist on a later occasion, or two psalms from different sources brought together at some time after their original composition.

.

Psalm 7. Prayer of a virtuous man under persecution.

Book	I
Number of verses	17
Key verse	9

Type of psalm	Lament
Possible original usage and setting	Both the Temple, or a more domestic venue are both possible
Including prayer or not	There is prayer, protest and prosecution!
Individual or Communal	Probably the words of an individual.
Date and author	There are a great variety of opinions. The identity of 'Cush the Benjaminite' is lost to antiquity.
Subsequent and Contemporary significance - Messianic indications	For Jew and Christian alike, the psalm has been a source of comfort even though more questions are posed than answers given.

As one commentator has said, this psalm feels anonymous!   To determine the venue, the date, the author or the context are now all beyond recall. There are here echoes of the man Job who expressed so many different emotions in his quest for justification, there is also the prayer of an innocent man. So, in this psalm there is both acceptance and revolt, as is so typical of the human condition when put to the test.

Very often throughout the Psalms, particularly in the Psalms of Lament, the writer or speaker whom we call the 'psalmist' is the plaintiff, who assumes himself to be innocent, rather than guilty. This is of course very different from the New Testament where Jesus Christ comes to forgive guilty sinners. This is a significant Old Testament / New Testament contrast.

This psalm brings up two issues, the first of being in the right as contrasted to being righteous, and the second the desire for justice contrasted to the desire for revenge (C.S. Lewis 1958).

Psalm 8. Lord, your world is amazing!

Book	I
Number of verses	9
Key verse	9

Type of psalm	Praise (or Hymn of creation)
Possible original usage and setting	In worship at the Feast of Tabernacles
Including prayer or not	Prayer and Praise
Individual or Communal	Communal
Date and author	Pre-exilic and many say written by David
Subsequent and Contemporary significance - Messianic indications	Throughout the centuries Psalm 8 has remained an extraordinarily popular hymn of praise and adoration.

Derek Kidner (1973) comments, "This is what a hymn should be". The psalm is celebration, joy, triumph, and is full of confidence. For many this is a prayer of adoration which looks back to the creation, which lives in the present and also looks forward especially in the prayers of children. This prayer psalm will have echoed down through the centuries and remains totally appropriate for private devotions or cathedral praise.

This is also a very modern hymn! It is an ecologically aware prayer in a world where the future of the planet is threatened by man's abuse of the environment.

This is a psalm that celebrates the glory, the power and the grace of God.

It is quoted in both the Old and New Testaments, e.g. Job 7.17, Ps. 144.3 Matthew 21.16 and Hebrews 2.6-8.

Psalm 9/10. God, the hope of the oppressed.

Book	I
Number of verses	20+18=38
Key verses	9.9& 9.19

Type of psalm	Lament predominantly, but really a mixed type.
Possible original usage and setting	Temple worship, and probably also in instruction.
Including prayer or not	Prayer and instruction
Individual or Communal	Both communal and individual
Date and author	Probably post-exilic written by a Temple priest or psalmist
Subsequent and Contemporary significance - Messianic indications	Psalm 9/10 reflects the human condition as well as any psalm.

Some Hebrew manuscripts and also the oldest Greek translation of the Old Testament regard Psalms 9 and 10 as one psalm. Still other manuscripts treat the two as separate psalms. There is a body of evidence to support each case. The material also expresses several different emphases e.g. there is lament and praise, thanksgiving and also prophecy and probably others.

It is a psalm which may reflect two sides of the character of King David, and indeed contrasting aspects of the general human condition.

On the technical side the psalm is acrostic, with some discrepancies perhaps indicating that the psalm has had a complex history. But the successive 22 letters of the Hebrew alphabet are mostly found as the initial letters of the verses in the Hebrew. The other acrostic psalms are 25, 34, 37, 111, 112, 119 and 145.

This is a psalm about the good and the bad, rewards and punishments.

Psalm 11. The Lord is my refuge.

Book	I
Number of verses	7
Key verse	5

Type of psalm	Praise
Possible original usage and setting	More likely personal rather than congregational
Including prayer or not	Not a prayer
Individual or Communal	An individual
Date and author	Little definitive evidence, scholars differ
Subsequent and Contemporary significance - Messianic indications	The plaintiff declares his confidence in God, and this continues to be the function of Psalm 11

This psalm expresses confidence in God. It is like Psalm 23 in this respect, along with other Psalms such as 4, 16, 27, 62 and 121. The penitent appears to trust God rather than to flee to the mountains as his associates seem to advocate. The psalm makes the point that flight is not the answer!

Clearly the psalm comes from a crisis situation, but we may only guess as to the nature of that crisis. The reader is left pondering the situation that gave rise to the ensuing debate between a troubled man and his friends with advice that he was not inclined to accept. Psalms like this remind us that the Psalter was written a long time ago and over a great period of time. The exact context is not known but the dilemma is sufficiently common to enable such a psalm to speak to ever so many dilemmas.

Psalm 12. We need God's help in a deceitful world.

Book	I
Number of verses	8
Key verses	5&6

Type of psalm	Lament
Possible original usage and setting	Not apparently appropriate for cult or liturgy but yet for worship – somewhat enigmatic!
Including prayer or not	Prayer and comment
Individual or Communal	Both individual and communal.
Date and author	Possibly a pre-exilic date and traditionally by King David
Subsequent and Contemporary significance - Messianic indications	This may well be a priest speaking to a congregation or a prophet declaring his message

The New Century Commentary by A.A. Anderson (1972) regards v. 5 as the focal point.

This short psalm has the ring of the 8th century prophets, men like Amos, Hosea and Micah. Here is the prayer of a contrite heart and an honest mind. The speaker knows his need, and declares the same before God and all the world.

These poignant verses are transparent in their integrity and in their honesty, and remain to this day a commentary on an often evil and corrupt world in which, nevertheless, God is in control.

These are the words of one who is at his wits end and knows that, when all human help fails, God is found to be there.

Psalm 13. Sometimes it is very dark!

Book	1
Number of verses	6
Key verse	1

Type of psalm	Lament
Possible original usage and setting	Personal prayer
Including prayer or not	Yes, a prayer
Individual or Communal	Individual with wide application still!
Date and author	Pre-exilic, possibly King David
Subsequent and Contemporary significance - Messianic indications	Petition remains essential in every generation for every believer

Psalm 13 is everyone's prayer, not every day but as occasion demands! Job prayed prayers like this, as did the prophets and the priests of Israel long ago, but so too do their contemporary equivalents feel led to pray equivalent prayers.

In fact, this is a very modern prayer about depression. And whereas prayer does not immediately relieve that awful condition, nevertheless prayer does in the end help many climb out of the hole even though at bad times there appears to be neither light nor relief. The message of Psalm 13 is to stay close to God and to seek his company. Yet these are the very things that the sufferer is unable to do! Here is a psalmist and a patient who long to stay close to God.

It is the prayer of friends, family and ministers that every sincere penitent who reads as far as v. 6 will come back to again and again.

Psalm 14. Are you really there Lord?

Book	1
Number of verses	7
Key verses	1&3

Type of psalm	Lament with overtones of both wisdom and prophecy
Possible original usage and setting	Comment on those and many other times
Including prayer or not	Not a prayer
Individual or Communal	Communal
Date and author	Post-exilic by an unknown psalmist
Subsequent and Contemporary significance - Messianic indications	Ours may well be a comparable world

Psalms 14 and 53 comprise a 'doublet'. These two psalms are almost identical, Psalm 14 in Book I and Psalm 53 in Book II. The vocabulary contains several pairs of words specifically identified as wisdom vocabulary i.e. good and bad, good and corrupt, fool and wise man.

Psalm 14 is classically a comment on those times but of course it is also a comment on many other periods of time. Here there are echoes of both the man Job and his railing against those who mistreated him. They did not understand him and his dilemma.

This is a sad psalm but also a very realistic assessment of the psalmist's era.

Psalm 15. Who can stand before God?

Book	I
Number of verses	5
Key verse	5 (2nd half)

Type of psalm	Praise with Wisdom overtones
Possible original usage and setting	Possibly used in Temple liturgy and in teaching
Including prayer or not	Only v. 1 is a prayer
Individual or Communal	Communal
Date and author	Pre-exilic with David as author a possibility
Subsequent and Contemporary significance - Messianic indications	This may well be a Messianic psalm looking forward to a messiah coming.

This psalm may well be messianic as no human being can reach the standards suggested here. There are, echoes here of both Psalms 1 and 26 but every psalm is unique - and Psalm 15 is no exception. The psalm lays down the qualities required for the perfect worshipper to attain; this may well be a messianic expectation rather than a human possibility!

The psalm deals with what believers are like outside and inside, and v. 2-5 are an intricate mixture of the inner self and what the observer sees from outside.

Compare both John's Gospel 14.1-6 and I John 2.1-9.

Psalm 16. The lines have fallen for me in pleasant places.

Book	I
Number of verses	11
Key verse	6

Type of psalm	Classified as Lament, but Praise also present
Possible original usage and setting	Temple liturgy
Including prayer or not	Prayer in v. 1 and 11, otherwise it is a comment
Individual or Communal	Individual within the liturgy
Date and author	Pre-exilic, a Davidic king or follower of David
Subsequent and Contemporary significance - Messianic indications	The quotations from this psalm in the Acts demonstrate how the early Church understood this psalm as referring to the Messiah to come

We can read this psalm as a prayer to God and a meditation about God. There are also echoes of the Wisdom literature.

The iconic v. 6 finds a place in Handel's Messiah. This accords well with an understanding of the psalm as a precious life secret. Psalm 16 defines two kinds of people: those who praise foreign gods and rely on false hopes and to those who worship the One and true God of Israel.

The final verse is also quoted in Acts 2, and is seen there as a prophecy of resurrection.

The psalm has the superscription of a miktam of David. The term 'miktam' is variously understood and very little can be understood from the superscription. It is a technical term which may refer to musical instruments.

Psalm 17. A plea for justice!

Book	I
Number of verses	15
Key verse	8

Type of psalm	Lament
Possible original usage and setting	Opinion varies, as to whether liturgical or not
Including prayer or not	Clearly Psalm 17 is a fervent prayer
Individual or Communal	Highly individual
Date and author	Both late pre-exilic and early post-exilic have been suggested
Subsequent and Contemporary significance - Messianic indications	This psalm may well be messianic, in that the goodness of the suppliant is extraordinary and beyond the capabilities of an ordinary person

Four Psalms (7, 17, 26 and 35) have all been classified as Psalms of Innocence and the term is self-explanatory. Much more difficult is to decide whether this psalm had a cultic liturgical origin or something much more personal. It has been suggested that the present psalm may have come from the Temple whereas an earlier version may have had more personal devotional usage.

Psalm 17 may be a prayer, a dream or an unrealistic illusion. Note particularly verse 15. And yet there is so much of this psalm to which everyone can relate. In a sense this is everyman's prayer.

The final verses are typical of the many times in the Psalter where terrible things are prayed for adversaries. This has given rise the term 'Cursing Psalms'. Were people in those days more vindictive or more honest? C. S. Lewis (1958) suggests that, what some psalmists wrote, many nowadays feel but do not express.

Psalm 18. The King's Prayer.

Book	I
Number of verses	50
Key verse	31

Type of psalm	Royal
Possible original usage and setting	A psalm of thanksgiving at an enthronement anniversary service
Including prayer or not	Prayer
Individual or Communal	One praying on behalf of all
Date and author	Probably pre-exilic, with David possibly the author, but more likely one of his successors (see v. 50)
Subsequent and Contemporary significance - Messianic indications	One of the earliest uses of the biblical tern 'rock' to describe God or a person God can trust – a strongly Messianic hymn. See Romans 15.9

Psalm 18 is far removed from common experience and yet in spite of this it rings with an authentic voice. The psalmist declares the power, the majesty, and the authority of God with a conviction that can span the centuries. These words resound with devotion and obedience and the devotion of the author makes the psalm messianic rather than contemporary. The psalm reveals a huge awareness of God and a great confidence in all that God can do.

Whether this is the earliest reference to God as a 'rock' is less important than the appreciation that the term is as relevant today as it has been throughout the centuries (v.31).

There is a close relationship between Psalm 18 and 2 Samuel 22.2-51. Whether or not David wrote the psalm is of much less importance than the wonderful insight into the King's spiritual life and the messianic vision wrought by repeated generations who have read, said and sung these words.

Psalm 19. God's creation and His Law.

Book	I
Number of verses	14
Key verses	7&14

Type of psalm	Praise of Creation
Possible original usage and setting	In the Temple, possibly at a New Year Festival
Including prayer or not	Not prayer, but praise
Individual or Communal	Communal
Date and author	Pre-exilic, with David named on the superscription
Subsequent and Contemporary significance - Messianic indications	Still used extensively in Christian praise, and in Jewish usage. Quoted in Romans 10.18

Psalm 19 is such an exciting psalm in three parts.

Verses 1-9 "Creation" reveals God's glory, v. 10-13 "The Law" reveals God's justice and v. 14 offers the worshipper the opportunity to speak with God. This 'Davidic' psalm allows a king to offer his adoration and his worship to the King of kings. The psalm also serves as an introduction to the much longer Psalm 119 which is also about God's law.

In addition to being quoted in the New Testament the psalm is also quoted in Handel's Messiah which was written in the seventeenth century.

Here is a psalm which has to do with the whole universe, the profundity of God's law and the totally personal relationship of an individual's heart.

The concluding prayer in v.14 has prefaced millions of sermons and can also be the preface of every believer's life every day – it is a formula for a good life!

Psalm 20. God save the King!

Book	I
Number of verses	9
Key verse	7

Type of psalm	Royal
Possible original usage and setting	Temple liturgy, praising God and honouring the king
Including prayer or not	Probably prayer
Individual or Communal	An individual (the king) is addressed alongside the prayer
Date and author	Late pre-exilic, by someone close to the king
Subsequent and Contemporary significance - Messianic indications	The king's Anointed One points at both the current dynasty and also towards a Messianic interpretation

Who is speaking is one question Psalm 20 raises. Although likely to have been in the Temple liturgy the psalm has the form of a loyal address to the sovereign, and the subject of the psalm is the king's relationship to God. The psalm is addressed to King David. Christians may well understand the psalm to refer to the One who would come.

Over the Christian centuries the psalm has enjoyed huge attention and has been variously interpreted. Today's interpretation may differ from that of 100, 1000 or 3000 years ago. It may still be taken as addressed to a King but equally it can be addressed to a good friend. The psalm may be prayed by anyone in any age for a friend or for a person needing the help of God. This is a psalm with wide applicability expressing both need and confidence.

Psalm 21. King by the grace of God.

Book	1
Number of verses	13
Key verse	7

Type of psalm	Royal (4th of 11)
Possible original usage and setting	Liturgy in the Temple, perhaps an annual enthronement occasion
Including prayer or not	Prayer and loyal address
Individual or Communal	It is all about the king, by a priest or a congregation
Date and author	Pre-exilic, about David or a Davidic king
Subsequent and Contemporary significance - Messianic indications	Regarded by many as messianic, but each reader makes their own decision

Psalms 20 and 21 are a pair, petition in psalm 20 and answer in psalm 21. The complex composition confirms for some that these psalms had a liturgical background.

It is reasonable to speculate that they were sung at some annual occasion, such as the anniversary of the king's enthronement, but this remains speculative.

Royal Psalms are about a king's relationship to God and to his people and to his enemies at the time the psalms were written. Messianic psalms are primarily about a forward reference to a coming Messiah. The two groups of psalms will inevitably overlap.

Psalm 21 is a prayer (v. 1-7) and a loyal address (v. 8-12) and there is strong support that such a psalm will have been commissioned by King David.

One commentator added the postscript that war is bad for everyone, simplistic perhaps, but let all the people say "Amen"!

Psalm 22. My God, my God why have you forsaken me?

Book	I
Number of verses	31
Key verse	1

Type of psalm	Lament, but also praise in v. 25-31, Mixed type
Possible original usage and setting	Temple use at the offering of a sacrifice. The speaker may be a Royal servant
Including prayer or not	Verses 1-21 are mainly prayer
Individual or Communal	Spoke or sung by an individual in the hearing of many
Date and author	Post exilic date by an unknown psalmist
Subsequent and Contemporary significance - Messianic indications	From New Testament times, onward this psalm has been understood messianically. This may not have been the original purpose of writing

This is probably the psalm most quoted in the New Testament. In all four Gospels some of verses 1, 7-8, 18 and 22 are quoted. Much later, verses from this psalm were quoted in Handel's Messiah. It may well be the most influential psalm upon the New Testament.

It is probably equally true that when first recorded, collected and used in the Temple it will have had more to do with contemporary events and less with the far future.

The two parts i.e. v. 1-21 and v. 22-31 are different. In the first, suffering is the subject, in the second, the subject is the deliverer who answers the prayers of the plaintiff, and God is declared as the Deliverer.

Psalm 23. The Lord is my shepherd.

Book	I
Number of verses	6
Key verse	1

Type of psalm	Praise, compare also Psalm 120
Possible original usage and setting	In the Temple at a thanksgiving occasion
Including prayer or not	Prayer and a declaration of trust in God
Individual or Communal	Individual, written in the singular with a universal application
Date and author	Pre-exilic traditionally ascribed to King David
Subsequent and Contemporary significance - Messianic indications	The best known psalm in the Christian era and most widely used for many worship occasions

The Church's favourite psalm because it makes a clear declaration of faith, allows a number of visual images, comforts, reassures and brings peace to troubled travellers along life's road.

Two biblical images are used for God – He is declared to be both shepherd and host at a heavenly (or earthly) banquet.

The psalm seems to be equally applicable to a huge cathedral and a bedside with anyone in extreme physical or emotional or spiritual need. Really, all things to all people. The Christian church has understood the psalm messianically and sees the ministry of Jesus fulfilling all the shepherd's roles.

In Romans 8.39 St Paul writes, "I am convinced that neither death nor life...will be able to separate us from the love of God". For millions of followers, this was first said in Psalm 23.

Psalm 24. He is the King of glory.

Book	I
Number of verses	10
Key verses	1 & 7

Type of psalm	Praise
Possible original usage and setting	Liturgical use in the Temple
Including prayer or not	About God, not a prayer to God
Individual or Communal	Communal
Date and author	Pre-exilic but after King Solomon
Subsequent and Contemporary significance - Messianic indications	Strongly Messianic psalm, anticipating a coming redeemer, often sung by Christians on Ascension Day.

Psalm 24 resonates with connections, to the Tabernacle, the Temple, to priestly worship, to liturgy and for many Christians is a profoundly Messianic psalm whose meaning is only completed with the Advent of Jesus Christ.

The psalm has three well defined sections, v. 1-2, 3-6 and 7-10.

The first section is a hymn of praise and can be compared with other hymns of praise like Psalms 100 and 150.

Verses 3-6 are an element of liturgy, possibly a sequence of prayer used in the Temple.

Verse 3 is the leader asking a question and v. 4 and 5 are the congregational response.

Verses 7-10 represents another change and may well be a Liturgy of the Gate as pilgrims arrived at City Gate or the Temple Gate.

With so much in so few verses, it explains why Psalm 24 is quoted so often in the New Testament. Could this psalm have been in Pilate's mind when he asked Jesus, "Are you a king?"

This psalm along with 10 other psalms is also quoted in Handel's Messiah.

Psalm 25. Doing it God's way.

Book	I
Number of verses	22
Key verses	7, 8 or 11

Type of psalm	Lament
Possible original usage and setting	Either liturgical or didactic purposes
Including prayer or not	Prayer of confession
Individual or Communal	Probably an individual psalm
Date and author	Post-exilic and anonymous
Subsequent and Contemporary significance - Messianic indications	This psalm is acrostic in the original Hebrew, with the 22 verses beginning with successive letters of the 22 letter alphabet.

The other acrostic psalms are 9, 10, 26, 34, 37, 111, 112, 119 and 145

A wonderful psalm to read in personal prayer and meditation. Whereas Psalm 1 was about two possible ways a man could go, Psalm 25 is about the right way.

The four main subjects, Kidner (1973) helpfully suggests, are enemies, guilt, guidance and trust. These are not treated separately but are woven into the fabric of the song and if the song can be learnt it becomes a powerful instrument in knowing God's leading. The 'way' is a repeated biblical theme in both the Old and New Testaments, for example, in Psalm 23 and in John's Gospel.

Psalms 25–30 all deal with the matter of life after death. There have been many opinions about this over the centuries – did the people of Israel anticipate an existence beyond the grave? Some say that following death all Israel and all the Old Testament simply expected SHEOL, a shadowy state with no expectation of continuing identity in any form, and yet other texts seem to suggest something more.

Psalm 26. Prayer of a blameless man.

Book	1
Number of verses	12
Key verse	11

Type of psalm	Lament written acrostically, like Ps 9,26,34,37,111,112,119 and 145.
Possible original usage and setting	A falsely accused individual seeks affirmation
Including prayer or not	A prayer or is it arrogant self-aggrandisement
Individual or Communal	Individual
Date and author	Pre-exilic, with some affirming David as author
Subsequent and Contemporary significance - Messianic indications	It may be that a Messianic interpretation is the only valid interpretation.

Psalm 26 presents a particular difficulty – no mere human was ever like this man! This psalmist is perfect, too good to be a real life sinful human being. Either the author is deluded or he is writing of one-to-come, a Messiah. There are several psalms which create the difficulty of being about, or written by a psalmist who is too good! The only possible explanation seems to be that the psalmist is not deluded but is expressing a prophetic hope in the kind-of-the-one- to-come, who would rescue mankind from the morass in which humanity found itself. And so, to this day there is no one who measures up to the standard set out by the psalmist, and no one can and we can only look beyond to the One Coming in triumph and in Judgement.

Nevertheless, the transparent integrity, the beautiful perfection, and the moral rectitude of the psalmist can lift our eyes beyond the frail and the human and the spoiled and look towards that to which we are being called.

Compare also parts of Psalm 89.

Psalm 27. God is my light and my salvation.

Book	1
Number of verses	14
Key verse	4

Type of psalm	Lament
Possible original usage and setting	Personal devotion
Including prayer or not	Prayer and meditation
Individual or Communal	Individual
Date and author	The psalm's date and author are not easily determined
Subsequent and Contemporary significance - Messianic indications	Like many other psalms this is a good hymn to sing

Psalm 27 shares some of the characteristics of a Royal Psalm, but is primarily a Lament. The psalm divides easily into parts, verses 1-6, and verses 7-22. So easily in fact that some have suggested that the two parts may originally have been two independent works, the first part a confession the second a Lament.

Later in the Psalter, psalms 114 and 115 present a similar possibility.

The overall lesson taught by the psalm is that life has its ups and its downs, and the key words appear to be *safe, enemies, heart, flight and afraid.*

Although there is little evidence for or against a particular date and author; the date may nevertheless be early pre-exilic and David may well have been the author. There appears to be no evidence to the contrary.

Psalm 28. Lord, hear my request.

Book	I
Number of verses	9
Key verse	9

Type of psalm	Lament
Possible original usage and setting	Temple worship
Including prayer or not	Including prayer
Individual or Communal	Individual and yet congregational
Date and author	Pre-exilic but probably the language and vocabulary indicate an author after David's time
Subsequent and Contemporary significance - Messianic indications	A priest speaks for the individual in congregational worship

Although this psalm is of the Lament type, it is reminiscent of the Royal psalms which deal with the relationship of God to his anointed one and the anointed one's relationship to the people. So often a psalm would fit in two categories, and often the decision seems almost arbitrary and leaves room for different opinions.

As was the case in the previous two psalms, 26 and 27, this one also is in two contrasting parts. Verses 1-5 are definitely lament whereas in v. 6–9 the mood lifts and the psalmist praises God.

These three psalms form something of a unit. All three are very personal, and they all express the fear of being cast out and counted with the wicked.

John 15.7 expresses something of the same in a more positive vein, "If my words abide in your heart, you can ask whatever you like and it will come true for you." (J.B. Philipps translation).

Psalm 29. The seven-fold voice of the Lord.

Book	I
Number of verses	11
Key verse	5

Type of psalm	Praise
Possible original usage and setting	Liturgy of the Temple, possibly at the last day of the Feast of Tabernacles, or Enthronement occasion
Including prayer or not	Not a prayer as such, it is praise!
Individual or Communal	Communal
Date and author	Pre-exilic and very old, originally Canaanite
Subsequent and Contemporary significance - Messianic indications	Psalm 29 remains exuberant praise to this very day!

According to Martini[16] (1990), the Archbishop of Milan, this psalm may well be the oldest in the entire five collections. He suggests that in its original form it may well have been used in a pagan celebration in a pagan community in Canaan. The psalm has great power which is emphasised by the three-fold parallelism in v. 3 and 4. In this psalm it is Israel's God Yahweh who is now being praised as God of the entire universe. He is God of Israel and is enthroned as their King.

Psalm 29 has also been called 'The Seven Thunder Psalm'. Here is Canaanite worship that has been re-worked into the salvation history of Israel. The name Yahweh has redeemed the pagan original. Hallelujah! The psalm calls its reader to recognise the primacy of God and to accept His peace.

---

[16] The archbishop follows the Roman Catholic numbering of the Psalms, and in his book this psalm is denoted as Psalm 28 on page 60. Martini CM (1990) What am I that you care for me? Praying with the Psalms. St Pauls Ireland.

Psalm 30. His anger is but for a moment.

Book	I
Number of verses	12
Key verse	5

Type of psalm	Praise with thanksgiving
Possible original usage and setting	Possibly after 164 BC at the Feast of Hanukkah
Including prayer or not	Prayer
Individual or Communal	This psalm is both singular and plural
Date and author	Late pre-exilic or early post-exilic, anonymous
Subsequent and Contemporary significance - Messianic indications	The later significance is that Psalm 30 has often found application as an aid to meditation.

The psalm immediately confronts the question of the afterlife, and many Christians will see much more of the New Testament than the Old in some of these verses. But this is an Old Testament scripture and must be read as such. The verses with their strong individualism may simply reflect the ups and downs that are an almost universal experience. "Weeping may tarry for the night, but joy comes in the morning." Whether such a prayer would or could have been prayer in Temple or synagogue is to be doubted and it may well be that the psalm is much more personal.

Psalm 31. My times are in your hands.

Book	I
Number of verses	24
Key verse	15

Type of psalm	Lament with thanksgiving also identified
Possible original usage and setting	Temple liturgy
Including prayer or not	Prayer
Individual or Communal	Strongly individual although liturgical
Date and author	Pre-exilic, David or a Davidic king possibly
Subsequent and Contemporary significance - Messianic indications	This psalm is extensively quoted in the New Testament

This psalm presents problems. Is it a unity or was it originally two or more psalms? What is the suppliant's problem? Is he ill, or falsely accused, or both? Nevertheless, many biblical characters call upon this psalm or rather they call upon the God of the one who wrote this psalm, and he delivered them.

This psalm is also one of the sources of the crucial Christian image of the 'rock' for the deliverer, and Saviour of the New Testament. Not only does Jesus compare Himself to a rock but he also assigns to Peter the high title of 'rock'.

The psalm is quoted in Jeremiah 6.25 and other verses, as well as in the New Testament in Luke 23.46. Psalm 71 also opens with the substance of the first three verses.

This psalm is often read in Christian worship in church but it is probably in personal and private devotion that the psalm finds its most appropriate applications.

Psalm 32. Forgiveness, repentance and instruction.

Book	I
Number of verses	11
Key verse	1

Type of psalm	Wisdom, 2nd of 11 Wisdom psalms
Possible original usage and setting	Instruction rather than worship more likely
Including prayer or not	Prayer and instruction
Individual or Communal	Individual with general application
Date and author	Post exilic possibly with an earlier original
Subsequent and Contemporary significance - Messianic indications	As a Wisdom type psalm this would indicate universal application and later Psalm 32 has become one of the 7 Christian Penitential Psalms i.e. Psalms 6,32,38,51,102,130 and 145.

Psalm 32 is difficult to classify. It is a Wisdom psalm, yet it also deals with repentance and forgiveness. It is, for Christians, a penitential psalm which has been used to confess sin and acknowledge dependence upon God for forgiveness. The psalm can be understood to imply that sin produces suffering, and for some that suffering is a sign that sin has been committed. In some fundamentalist churches this view is still held.

It is, however, the notes of wisdom and the declarations of forgiveness that are most stressed and most appreciated in this psalm.

The need for prayer and for instruction are universal among Christians and so this psalm is read and re-read by the faithful throughout their lives of faith.

Psalm 33. Rejoice in the Lord or My soul waits for the Lord.

Book	I
Number of verses	22
Key verse	8

Type of psalm	Praise, with echoes of traditional Wisdom
Possible original usage and setting	For use in worship possibly at Autumnal festival
Including prayer or not	Not prayer but thanksgiving and praise to God
Individual or Communal	Communal
Date and author	Post-exilic by anonymous author
Subsequent and Contemporary significance - Messianic indications	Praise and joy in creation are the keynotes

The right way to approach God is with prayer in your heart and on your lips! This is one of the lessons of Psalm 33. There are similarities here to Psalms 8 and 24. Although Matthew 28.18-20 (which says, "Go into the world and share your faith") is not a quotation from the psalm there is nevertheless a similarity in the meaning between the two. Here is a psalm which confirms a believer's faith. It is to be read when doubt threatens and when the skies are grey! As the words become familiar, so the believer is strengthened, and the enquirer is encouraged to read on. There are echoes of other psalms and other Bible passages e.g. Psalm 150.

A story line is not dominant and there is little continuous narrative. These two factors make it hard to memorize and difficult to identify. But the real strength of this song is that it crosses continents, speaks to those of any faith (and perhaps none), and is as true today as the day when it was written.

Psalm 34. O taste and see that the Lord is good.

Book	I
Number of verses	22
Key verse	8

Type of psalm	Praise, but with echoes of Lament in v.11ff
Possible original usage and setting	For instruction, possibly group or class lessons. It is acrostic in structure
Including prayer or not	This psalm is not a prayer
Individual or Communal	Singular in v.1 f, but plural in v.11f
Date and author	Post-exilic, author unknown
Subsequent and Contemporary significance - Messianic indications	Psalms 33 and 34 are similar. Instruction seems to be the key note but specific significance difficult to define.

Psalm 34 is more intimate than Psalm 33 to which it is otherwise similar in message and content. Verse 8 in particular has come into Christian usage in the Sacrament of the Lord's Supper.

The psalm is quoted twice by the author of 1 Peter which illustrates the importance of the Psalter to both Jews and Christians, and in both the Old and New Testaments.

Here is a psalm which has the echoes of a class situation with the instructor both proclaiming his personal faith and consequently urging his students to do likewise. This is among the most dynamic and vibrant of the teaching psalms and very like some of the Wisdom type e.g. Psalm 1.

Psalm 35. I am your deliverance.

Book	I
Number of verses	28
Key verse	17

Type of psalm	Lament but not all in a minor key!
Possible original usage and setting	Perhaps a priest on behalf of the king in Temple worship
Including prayer or not	Prayer and proclamation
Individual or Communal	Individual or spoken on behalf of an individual
Date and author	Early post exilic or late pre-exilic
Subsequent and Contemporary significance - Messianic indications	Echoes of the book of Job and v. 19 is quoted in John 15.25

Some have expressed the view that Psalm 35 was originally composed as three psalms i.e. v. 1-10, 11–18 and 19–28. They are all in lament mode but seem to relate to different situations. There appear to be three distinct petitions. There are those who contend against the psalmist, those who are false witnesses against him and those gossipy malcontents who want to discredit the psalmist. There are three corresponding promises of deliverance.

Whereas the psalmist was a good man who prayed for his adversaries and fasted when they were sick, no matter what rumours they were spreading about him, his enemies sought to discredit him at every opportunity.

God rescues the beleaguered psalmist who in all three sections of the psalm declares his praise and thanks to God his deliverer (v. 9, 18 and 29).

Psalm 36. Man sins and God rescues.

Book	I
Number of verses	12
Key verse	6

Type of psalm	Predominantly a Lament but the marks of other types also evident.
Possible original usage and setting	A priest at worship, or a teacher in a class or an individual praying alone – all are possible
Including prayer or not	Prayer in part
Individual or Communal	Individual or for an individual by a teacher
Date and author	Late rather than early is the majority opinion
Subsequent and Contemporary significance - Messianic indications	A lament with accompanying thankfulness is appropriate for both Jews and Christians v.1 is quoted in Romans 3.18

Verse 4 is reminiscent of Amos 8.5, and other verses are reminiscent of other psalms. There are echoes of Psalm 1 and 14.

There is deep gratitude in the heart of the psalmist and this can be echoed by every reader. This is a good psalm to meditate upon because it takes the reader on a journey from contemplating wickedness to appreciating God's goodness and giving thanks for it, and concludes by warning the worshipper of the dangers of evil.

The psalm like some others is written in a cyclical style.

"The words of his mouth" referring to the wicked are contrasted to the thrice repeated phrase "thy steadfast love" of God for the believer. The wicked one sets himself in a way that is not good.

This is at least part of the meaning and the message of Psalm 36.

Psalm 37. Trust in the Lord and do good.

Book	I
Number of verses	40
Key verse	27

Type of psalm	Wisdom psalm, there are 11 in the Psalter and at least 9 acrostic psalms of which this is one. Others are Ps 9/10,26,34,37,111,112,119, and 145
Possible original usage and setting	Used for teaching by the Wise men rather than by the prophets or the priests
Including prayer or not	Instruction rather than prayer
Individual or Communal	Communal – this is wisdom for all
Date and author	Exilic possibly fourth century BC
Subsequent and Contemporary significance - Messianic indications	Verse 11 is reminiscent of the 3rd Beatitude "Blessed are the meek for they shall inherit the earth." Matthew 5.5

Here is a psalm that could be equally comfortable in the Book of Proverbs. Many of the hallmarks of the Wisdom writings are clearly seen in this and other Wisdom type psalms. Examples of such phrases are 'refrain from anger', and 'the wicked will be no more' and 'depart from evil and do good'. Pairs of words typical of wisdom include, 'good and evil', 'wicked and righteous', 'anger and wrath' and 'young and old'. One suggestion is that the climax is 'the righteous belong to God and the wicked will be no more'.

The Wisdom route to God is often different from that of the priests and their acolytes. It is no accident that the Wise men were a breed of teacher whose influence extended beyond the geographical and religious limits of Israel.

Psalm 38. Confessions of a sick and sinful man.

Book	I
Number of verses	22
Key verse	18

Type of psalm	Lament
Possible original usage and setting	Personal reflection, a meditation on sadness and sickness
Including prayer or not	Prayer
Individual or Communal	Individual
Date and author	Post-exilic, perhaps in the prophet Jeremiah's time
Subsequent and Contemporary significance - Messianic indications	The content of Psalm 38 remains contemporary and significant to this very day! This is a human condition in every age. Many Christians will want to understand psalm 38 messianically.

Whereas the penitent in Psalm 37 was an innocent man unjustly condemned by wicked and evil men, the penitent in Psalm 38 is a guilty sinner in need of forgiveness. He understands his suffering and illness to be the consequence of his sin which was the universal assumption in those pre-Christian times. Psalm 38 is another of the Seven Penitential Psalms, the other six being Psalms 6, 32, 51,102,130 and 143. The Christian Church has, for many centuries, understood these psalms in that light. Guilty sinners may come to Jesus Christ for forgiveness and restoration in the sight of God. This is the contrast between their fate and the fate of the unfortunate Job who was unable to have the confidence that he could be restored to a right relationship with God.

Here the psalmist was hurting through pain, loneliness and depression, although depression is not a biblical word. The penitent has sunk very low and yet still clings tenuously to his belief in God and does believe that God can help him and will do so. Verse 21 remains to this day a prayer said by many penitent sinners.

Psalm 39. Lord, let me know my end.

Book	I
Number of verses	13
Key verses	12, 13

Type of psalm	Lament
Possible original usage and setting	Possibly private devotional use, not at public worship
Including prayer or not	Includes some prayer e.g. v.4
Individual or Communal	Individual
Date and author	Possibly fifth century BC
Subsequent and Contemporary significance - Messianic indications	In any age this is a powerful devotional aid

All of the psalms were originally for speaking, singing, and reading aloud. They are essentially for oral use. Psalm 39 is no exception and has been called 'a beautiful elegy' implying the spoken word. There is also some kinship here with the Wisdom literature. Certainly, this psalm is more intimate than much liturgy.

And yet v. 12 has been adopted for responsive prayer, but then v.13 raises the difficult thought, *"Look away from me, that I may know gladness, before I depart and be no more"*. To some hard questions there are no easy answers.

This psalm contemplates the fundamental question of why is God interested, involved and concerned about man? The psalm expresses for every penitent the intention to come back to the Father. Indeed Psalm 39 expresses the longings in so many prodigal sons and daughters.

Psalm 40. I waited patiently for the Lord.

Book	I
Number of verses	17
Key verses	3 or 17

Type of psalm	Lament, but with thanksgiving and praise – this is a mixed type psalm
Possible original usage and setting	Liturgical use
Including prayer or not	Verses 1–4 are praise, the remainder prayer
Individual or Communal	Individual but in a corporate setting!
Date and author	Post-exilic with author anonymous
Subsequent and Contemporary significance - Messianic indications	Psalm 40 was written to meet an ever-present need and still meets it.

A psalm of different moods, in v. 7–10 there is committed discipleship, in 14–16 there is reaction against injustice, in 1–3 and 4–5 there is waiting upon God. There is lament but there is also expressed a great confidence in the power of God. The message to the unfolding generations is "the Lord has given me a new song."

What God has done, God can do is the repeated meaning of this psalm for each succeeding generation.

There are close connections between Psalms 40 and 70 but also with Micah 6.6 and v. 6-8 are quoted in Hebrews 10.5-9

C.S. Lewis (1958) points out that the words in v. 15 mean that it is not only the suffering of the righteous but also of the guilty that Christ takes upon himself when he plumbed the depths on our account.

Psalm 41. Raise me up.

Book	I
Number of verses	12 (and the doxology at the end of Book I)
Key verse	10

Type of psalm	A Praise type psalm but with elements of lament
Possible original usage and setting	Temple worship
Including prayer or not	Prayer and praise with intercession
Individual or Communal	For each individual in a corporate setting
Date and author	Post-exilic
Subsequent and Contemporary significance - Messianic indications	The thanksgiving implies praise, but the pleading implies lament. This is a roller-coaster psalm.

With the mention of a 'bosom' friend who is less than loyal, the psalmist here reminds his readers of the man Job whose friends were not true friends. So, the psalm expresses need and subsequent thanksgiving, as God intervened to safe the suffering victim.

The message of the psalm is to keep trusting God in every adversity and then he will, in spite of that hardship, redeem the penitent sufferer who continues to do God's will.

The psalmist places great reliance upon the orthodox statement of faith: that the righteous will be rewarded and the wicked will perish. This is that same faith that Job railed against.

Psalm 41 finishes at v. 12 and this also ends Book I of the Psalter. When this collection was later joined with four other collections each collection had added a concluding doxology – a short hymn of praise which has here been numbered as psalm 41.13.

Psalm 42 and 43. Why are you downcast O my soul?

Book	II
Number of verses	11+5
Key verse	5

Type of psalm	Lament
Possible original usage and setting	Used in liturgy although probably not in the Temple.
Including prayer or not	Prayer and meditation
Individual or Communal	Individual
Date and author	Either exilic or post-exilic, anonymous author
Subsequent and Contemporary significance - Messianic indications	The imagery has fascinated both Jewish and Christian believers down through the centuries

This is the first two psalms of the second collection i.e. Psalms 42–72. This highly individualistic psalm is both prayer and conversation. The dialogue being between the psalm and the worshipper. There is regret, almost pain, that he is now estranged from God. There is passionate longing for a restoration of the relationship.

The psalm(s) are thought to have originally been one for four reasons:

1. There is no title for Psalm 43
2. There is the common refrain used in both see v. 42.5, 11 and 43.5.
3. There is the same poetic metre and thought throughout.
4. Similarities of subject and vocabulary.

Even if this psalm was not written in the exile in Babylon the language and mood suggest exile, loneliness and the plaintiff longing for 'hearth and home'.

Loneliness and pathos dominate Psalm 42/43 and it remains one of the most emotional psalms in the entire collection.

Psalm 44. Lament of a defeated nation.

Book	II
Number of verses	26
Key verse	9

Type of psalm	Lament with a prophetic sound
Possible original usage and setting	Liturgical use to expunge pent up wrath
Including prayer or not	Angry prayer!
Individual or Communal	Communal with some first person singular verses
Date and author	Post exilic perhaps sixth century BC
Subsequent and Contemporary significance - Messianic indications	In any generation, any nation and any king could write this hymn. It is anger and faith woven together.

There is enormous energy in this psalm. The king or leader who writes it cannot understand why God has let them down. He feels that they have not been sinful or disobedient and yet in contrast to the way He, God, blessed and provided for their predecessors He has not done the same and they with him feel let down.

Psalm 44 has echoes of both the man Job who felt that God had let him down, and echoes of the anger of the prophets like Isaiah, "Why Lord?", they scream.

Defeat is never sweet!

In this psalm, there are bitter/sweet lessons to be learnt on a personal as well as a national level. There is a place for angry prayer and God has heard it all before!

Verse 22 is quoted in Romans 8.36, "*Nay for thy sake we are slain all the day long, and accounted as sheep for the slaughter.*"

Psalm 45. A love poem and a royal wedding.

Book	II
Number of verses	17
Key verse	7b

Type of psalm	Royal
Possible original usage and setting	Used in worship on a special occasion, such as a royal wedding or anniversary
Including prayer or not	Praise not prayer
Individual or Communal	Spoken by an individual, or for an individual for the people
Date and author	Little agreement
Subsequent and Contemporary significance - Messianic indications	The description of a most excellent king will have allowed Christians to understand the hymn messianically.

This psalm is reminiscent of the biblical love story the Song of Songs. The king was not only the political but also the religious leader of the people of Israel. As such this was a fitting hymn to be sung in the Temple in Jerusalem, on a special occasion such as an anniversary or occasional celebration or even at the marriage of the king and his queen. It will have been the messianic interpretation that will have assured the psalm of a place in the Psalter. The passage in Ephesians 5.32,33 is clearly an echo of the words of Psalm 45. This is yet a further example of how many times the Book of Psalms is used by the writers of the New Testament and clearly they all knew the psalter well.

For Christians, there are two levels at which to interpret the words of this psalm: either as the historic record of the love of a king and his queen, or as the fulfilment in the New Testament of that which was looked forward to in the Old Testament.

Psalm 46. Be still and know that I am God.

Book	II
Number of verses	11
Key verse	10

Type of psalm	Praise
Possible original usage and setting	In the Jerusalem Temple, perhaps at Enthronement occasion
Including prayer or not	Praise rather than prayer, but really devotional
Individual or Communal	Communal for all the people
Date and author	Pre-exilic perhaps by a Temple musician
Subsequent and Contemporary significance - Messianic indications	For Jew and Christian this is a core psalm. Martin Luther in the sixteenth century AD made this one of the definitive praises of the Reformation in his hymn 'Ein feste Burg'.

This is a battle hymn full of the images of peace! This is a hymn from yesterday and for today, giving assurance for tomorrow.

These three Psalms, 46, 47 and 48, are about the City of God. These are all hymns about God's Kingship over all the earth. Zion can be variously understood as both a synonym for Jerusalem and as the dwelling place of God whether in earthly or in heavenly locations. Zion is also the dwelling place of the Ark of God in the Temple.

Psalm 46 is full of the images of war and yet is definitively a hymn of peace. The original psalm may well have been part of the inspiration of the City of God to be found in Revelation Chapter 21.

Psalm 47. Our God is King of all.

Book	II
Number of verses	9
Key verse	7

Type of psalm	Praise, almost fanatical
Possible original usage and setting	Possibly sung at the Annual Enthronement occasion when God was recognised as the Supreme Ruler of Israel and the world.
Including prayer or not	A hymn not a prayer
Individual or Communal	Communal praise
Date and author	Like Psalm 46 and 48, Psalm 47 may also be pre-exilic.
Subsequent and Contemporary significance - Messianic indications	Blatantly for Jew and Christian this psalm is understood as looking forward to one who is to come, whom Christians know as Jesus Christ.

This psalm is unrestrained praise and adoration of God. Here there is neither doubt nor division, Yahweh the God of Israel is THE God of all the earth by virtue of being creator and sustainer. For Christians, this psalm is not an anticipation of the Christian doctrine of the Ascension, but rather the realisation of that the life and work of Jesus Christ are a continuation and the final part of salvation history begun with the earliest records of God's activity in the Old Testament.

Are psalms like this one which speak of the reign and rule of God over all the nations, a prayer or a prophecy or a remote possibility if conceived in earthly terms? In the face of fundamentalist Islam there is much for Christians to ponder about the object of missionary activity.

Psalm 48. City of God.

Book	II
Number of verses	14
Key verse	8

Type of psalm	Praise, third of trilogy of Psalms 46, 47 and 48
Possible original usage and setting	Possibly used at the Feast of Tabernacles in the Jerusalem Temple.
Including prayer or not	Verses 9-11 are a prayer, the remaining verses are a hymn
Individual or Communal	Communal praise
Date and author	Possibly pre-exilic like Psalms 46 and 47
Subsequent and Contemporary significance - Messianic indications	Saint Augustine of Hippo in the third century AD, one of the earliest and one of the greatest of the early church fathers wrote a book called 'City of God'.

The City of God is a biblical image throughout much of the Bible not least in the books of Genesis and Revelation. The history of salvation moves forward through the centuries towards the City of God when God's rule will be throughout the new heaven and the new earth. It is unlikely that Psalm 48 had these ultimate expectations when it was written but rather had much more to do with their current life situation in Israel. However subsequent generations progressively realised the messianic expectations of the 'City of God' image.

Throughout these three psalms, Zion is continually realised as much more than Jerusalem, the mere earthly capital of Judah.

Psalm 49. Man's destiny depends on God, not on his riches.

Book	II
Number of verses	20
Key verse	12

Type of psalm	Wisdom. 4th of 11 Wisdom psalms. The others are 1,32,37,49,73,78,112,119,127,128 and 133.
Possible original usage and setting	For instruction, rather than worship
Including prayer or not	Not a prayer, more like a lesson
Individual or Communal	Communal
Date and author	Post-exilic
Subsequent and Contemporary significance - Messianic indications	Wisdom is very much the language of every age as well as all people and all faiths.

There were three groups of religious experts in Old Testament times. There were the prophets, such as Isaiah; the priests, who were responsible for the services and sacrifices in the Temple; and the Wise men who wrote the Books of Job and Proverbs and some of the Psalms. Psalm 49 is an example of the writing of the Wise men. They were concerned with the matters of riches and poverty, with foolishness and wisdom, with rewards and punishments and particularly here with life and death and what happens after death. The Wise men of Israel were also in dialogue with Wise men of the surrounding nations.

The particular issue in this psalm is that even very rich people are parted from their wealth when they die. The psalmist argues that those who have made their peace with God will be content whatever the after-life. In the Old Testament, there are only a very limited number of references to life beyond the grave. Psalm 49.15 seems to be one of these where the teaching of the New Testament is anticipated.

Psalm 50. Speech from the throne of heaven.

Book	II
Number of verses	23
Key verse	23

Type of psalm	Praise and prophecy and theophany. *
Possible original usage and setting	Prophetic utterance possibly on the occasion of a Covenant Renewal ceremony
Including prayer or not	Not a prayer
Individual or Communal	For all the people to hear
Date and author	Pre-exilic possibly in King Josiah's reign in 6th C BC
Subsequent and Contemporary significance - Messianic indications	In any generation, this is about covenant responsibility by the people of God, originally for Jews and subsequently Jesus confronted his hearers in the same vein. And to this day does so.

If prophecy is the dominant idea then theophany is the supporting medium. God speaking, appearing, manifesting Himself and being powerfully present to the worshippers through the lips and perhaps also by the pen of the prophet. God is judge in this psalm (especially in verses 8, 9, 12-15, and16). God summons the earth represented by Israel his special envoy.

There are very few psalms as militant as Psalm 50, but the huge confidence this powerful hymn exudes is infectious for good and for God!

*The theophany here is God appearing and speaking, presumably through the mouth of a prophet like Moses. See Exodus 19.25 and chapter 20 and the prophets like Isaiah and Amos. Theophany is literally an appearance of God.

Psalm 51. Have mercy upon me, O God.

Book	II
Number of verses	19
Key verse	10

Type of psalm	It is a Lament, many would say, THE Lament in the Psalter. Psalms 51-64 are all laments.
Possible original usage and setting	This will have been a psalm of the Temple, for liturgical use, for confession and absolution
Including prayer or not	Prayer and responses
Individual or Communal	Individual and communal
Date and author	The language is that of the eighth century BC. Traditionally written by King David.
Subsequent and Contemporary significance - Messianic indications	Psalm 51 expresses Jewish and Christian believers' confessions for 3000 years and consequentially has become the foremost Penitential Psalm.

The words 'mercy', 'transgressions', 'wash me', 'cleanse me', 'purge me', indeed the whole vocabulary of this seminal psalm, are at the core of Christian forgiveness and confirm the messianic interpretation of this above all other psalms. The other six penitential psalms are numbers 6, 32, 38, 102, 130 and 143.

Psalm 51 represents the most vital bridge between the Old and New Testaments. Perhaps guilt and salvation are the two poles. But indeed, the whole vocabulary of this responsive prayer has become the essential words by which Christians express their needs and ask for their renewal.

Verse 4 is quoted in Romans 3.4 when Paul quotes directly, "That thou mayest be justified in thy words and prevail when thou art judged".

Psalm 52. You wicked man!

Book	II
Number of verses	9
Key verse	7

Type of psalm	Lament, with thanksgiving in v.8-9
Possible original usage and setting	If this is a private lament then personal use is more likely than liturgical use before a congregation. Aim: to cure law breakers.
Including prayer or not	Prayer included
Individual or Communal	Individual
Date and author	Pre-exilic. Possibly King David is the author.
Subsequent and Contemporary significance - Messianic indications	Psalm 52 seems more tied to its original context than many others and therefore has less subsequent or Christian application.

The contrast here is between the law breaker of v. 1-4 and the godly one of v. 7, 8 and 9. The fate of the godless is contrasted with the one who laughs at him. Whether or not this is a commendation for the righteous man is another question.

It would be hard to hear this psalm if you were the accused and supposedly godless one. It might too be very difficult to address the rich, powerful, successful but evil man if you were the supposedly virtuous one.

Either way Psalm 52 presents difficulties both for the speaker and the hearer, for good and bad, for virtuous and for the one being taken to task!

Psalm 53, as per Psalm 14

Psalms 14 and 53 are a couple i.e. the texts of both are almost identical and occur in separate collections. Books I and II, each contain copy.

Psalm 54. O Lord hear my prayer.

Book	II
Number of verses	7
Key verse	4

Type of psalm	Lament
Possible original usage and setting	Perhaps Temple liturgical worship
Including prayer or not	Prayer with comment in last verse
Individual or Communal	Individual originally
Date and author	This is a psalm where opinion varies, some say early pre-exilic, possibly written by King David, whereas others disagree.
Subsequent and Contemporary significance - Messianic indications	This poignant little poem will have met the need of worshippers ever since the day it was written, not least to this very day.

In summary Psalm 54 is a petition (v.1-2), a complaint (v.3), an expression of trust (v.4-5) and a vow of thanksgiving (v.6-7). Verses 1-3 are prayer while v.4-7 are confident assurance. This was the case when the psalm was written and wonderfully this is still how it can be read.

The experts are not agreed on the history of this psalm, neither its date, origin nor its author. This does not in any way invalidate the devotional value that it has been to countless generations of sincere believers and serious enquirers.

Psalm 55. Cast your burden upon the Lord.

Book	II
Number of verses	23
Key verse	22

Type of psalm	Lament
Possible original usage and setting	Not for Temple or synagogue use but probably more for personal devotion
Including prayer or not	Prayer and exhortation
Individual or Communal	Individual
Date and author	Probably early post-exilic by unknown distressed psalmist
Subsequent and Contemporary significance - Messianic indications	Quoted in the New Testament, as are so many psalms. Verse 22 is quoted in 1 Peter 5.7

The frequent cross references between psalms and the New Testament demonstrates how well the writers of the New Testament knew the Book of Psalms.

In Psalm 55 there are at least two adversaries: the first is the psalmist's enemy (v.2-8, and 16-19), the second his own close friend (v.12-14, 20-21). There is perhaps also civil unrest (v.9-11).

Here the words of the king, or the words that the psalmist puts into the king's mouth, makes this a difficult psalm to understand. What is very clear is that many times the Psalms deal with suffering and the sufferer. It can be the king, or the nation Israel, or for Christians the suffering that the Messiah was to go through many centuries later.

This is the suffering that we will all in some way, at some point, have to experience. These songs prepare believers in every age for what is universal human experience.

Psalm 56. In God I trust, without a fear.

Book	II
Number of verses	13
Key verse	11

Type of psalm	Lament
Possible original usage and setting	This could be the response of the faithful after prayers of confession and repentance
Including prayer or not	Prayer
Individual or Communal	Primarily individual
Date and author	Possibly early post-exilic, and the author remains anonymous
Subsequent and Contemporary significance - Messianic indications	This will be the kind of psalm to which Jesus will have turned in his agony, and so for many Christians there is a Messianic interpretation.

Three concerns dominate this psalm – lament that the psalmist's enemies are never off his back, that they continually seek his downfall, and then thanksgiving that God takes care of him.

Psalm 56 is a lament that his enemies are so wicked, an expressed wish that God would vanquish them, and thanksgiving that God is so good to him.

Verse 8 makes a fascinating study in the variety of different words used to express God keeping record of his sufferings: NIV record; RSV bottle, GNB wineskin, Petersen's Messenger, ledger.

C.S. Lewis (1958) designates Psalm 56 as one of the "cursing psalms" along with such others as Psalms 23, 58, 69, 109, 137, 139 and 143. (pg. 9-19 and 99-108) In all of these the psalmist wishes awful retribution on all those who torment God's servants. Lewis explains that the psalms tell it as it is, and so often they advocate what modern Christians might feel in their hearts but would be ashamed to confess!

Psalm 57. Saved to sing.

Book	II
Number of verses	11
Key verse	9

Type of psalm	Lament (with thanksgiving)
Possible original usage and setting	Private worship and meditation
Including prayer or not	Prayer
Individual or Communal	Individual
Date and author	Late pre-exilic, possibly David or a Davidic king
Subsequent and Contemporary significance - Messianic indications	Messianic: Many Christians will understand their faith as the completion of v.3

There appears to be a relationship between Psalm 57.7-11 and Psalm 106.1-5. The majority of scholars would see Psalm 57 as the earlier with Psalm 106 v1-5 deriving from it.

The details of the subscription/heading do not quite accord with the biblical record but some scholars see the connection and therefore ascribe authorship to David.

The prayer opens in v.1 with the common biblical image of taking refuge under the wings of God and continues to provide solace for Jew and Christian in any need.

Indeed, the psalm translates easily into a Christian prayer of confession, absolution and thankfulness to God. The movement from v. 1, "Be merciful to me O God" to v. 11, "Be exalted O God, above the heavens" is a validation of the exercise of prayer, and is wonderful.

Psalm 58. Surely there is a God who judges the earth?

Book	II
Number of verses	11
Key verse	11

Type of psalm	Lament, perhaps a national lament
Possible original usage and setting	Perhaps in public worship, perhaps a national act of penitence seeking God's favour.
Including prayer or not	Prayer
Individual or Communal	Communal
Date and author	The language appears to be post-exilic although some ascribe authorship to David
Subsequent and Contemporary significance - Messianic indications	Some commentators see an echo of this psalm in Matthew 11.16,17 and also in Luke 6.46

This is another cursing psalm which Christians find difficult (see Psalm 56 and others). These psalms, which seek punishment on evil doers in very exact terms, are difficult to pray without feeling hypocritical and judgemental. Nevertheless, they are true reflections on human feelings and reactions.

Saint Augustine in the fourth century AD and Dietrich Bonhoeffer (1953) in the twentieth century AD both saw Christ speaking through this psalm. It was Bonhoeffer who realised that these psalms can become *our* prayers only because they were Jesus' prayers!

These psalms are not easy to pray partly because Christians are sometimes subject to unchristian passions rages and tempers!

Psalm 58 is hard to translate and this explains why there are considerable variations in the different Bible translations.

Psalm 59. Protect me, O my God.

Book	II
Number of verses	17
Key verse	6,7 (repeated at 14,15)

Type of psalm	Lament
Possible original usage and setting	The structure suggests that this psalm had come to be used in Temple worship.
Including prayer or not	Prayer included
Individual or Communal	Perhaps originally an individual lament but later incorporated into a Temple liturgy
Date and author	Early date and some say was written by David before he was king
Subsequent and Contemporary significance - Messianic indications	The images and language of this psalm are foreign to contemporary worship forms and vocabulary

This psalm has been variously interpreted. Some recognising a close link with King David while others seeing nothing of this. Whether it is an individual lament or a national one is also an open question and for this reason some have suggested that this is a composite psalm with v.1-10 and 11-17 being originally separate hymns. Is the enemy beyond or within? Is the enemy singular or plural? Is this civil disobedience or an external threat? The psalm seems ambiguous in various ways. It has been suggested that the suppliant could be either an old man, a little demented, or a leader at his wits end as to what is best to do.

This is not a straightforward psalm to either understand or apply. However, like many of the more complicated psalms, Psalm 59 finally comes around to the uninhibited praise of God in the final two verses. Dr Felix Chingota of Chancellor College, University of Malawi pointed out these circular phenomena which occur in many psalms (personal communication).

Psalm 60. Both defeat and deliverance.

Book	II
Number of verses	12
Key verse	12

Type of psalm	Lament
Possible original usage and setting	Liturgical worship at times of crisis
Including prayer or not	Prayer for help!
Individual or Communal	Communal
Date and author	Post-exilic, sixth century BC or later
Subsequent and Contemporary significance - Messianic indications	This is a nation in conflict. Successes and defeats are part of warfare.

Neither the story of this psalm, nor its measurement, is simple to discern. It is almost as if some verses have been lost or missed out. Psalm 60 may have had an older source document. A battle has been lost (v.1-5) and the mood seems to oscillate. In v.1-3 there is a low ebb, in v. 4 optimism is rising, and by v.5-11 the mood is dark again. Finally, in v.12, hope is restored and faith declared. Historians find it difficult to identify these verses with any exact historical period.

Psalm 60 is a low point in the nation's wellbeing and its morale.

This psalm is not only a reflection on Israel's troubled history but also on the course of personal human life. Here is a psalm about some ill-defined historical period and also the reflection of many a pilgrim's wandering. In personal life, victories and defeats are part of every pilgrimage.

In this psalm, the meaning and the message are not easily separated any more than they are in life.

Psalm 61. God is my sure refuge.

Book	II
Number of verses	8
Key verse	3

Type of psalm	Lament
Possible original usage and setting	Personal intercession and thanksgiving
Including prayer or not	Prayer
Individual or Communal	Individual
Date and author	Pre-exilic; possibly King David
Subsequent and Contemporary significance - Messianic indications	The 'rock' reference in v.2 will have echoes throughout the Old and New Testaments and Messianic implications for Christians. See also Ps. 62

As we wrestle to understand the Psalter we do well to remember that the psalms were all written in another language, in the Middle East, and most of them more than 2,700 years ago! These constraints need to temper our enthusiasm for certainty and accuracy. It is marvellous that there is access to the results of research and discovery over the centuries.

Psalm 61 is an Individual Lament but v.6-7 seem incongruous.

Hope is an essential element of many psalms and when David and his successors felt their hearts weak they were afraid. They turned to God, and searchers in every generation can come to this same holy song which teaches that trusting God in every situation is the appropriate response. His hope was strengthened and so too can the weakness of contemporary believers be made strong.

Psalm 62. In God alone!

Book	II
Number of verses	12
Key verse	6

Type of psalm	Lament, but also a psalm of trust, with wise sayings
Possible original usage and setting	Both public worship and private devotion are appropriate uses, and in teaching.
Including prayer or not	Includes prayer
Individual or Communal	Individual, and by each individual in a congregation
Date and author	Late pre-exilic or early post-exilic, anonymous
Subsequent and Contemporary significance - Messianic indications	Psalm 62.12 is quoted in Jeremiah 17.10, Revelation 2.23 and 22.12 "You will reward each person according to what he has done"

It is not immediately apparent who the psalmist is or whom he is addressing! He appears to be a somewhat remote figure addressing an undefined audience. As in Psalm 61 the image of the rock is again cited in this psalm. The repeated refrain (in v.1-2 and 5-6) suggests either a choral recitation or two separate and distinct audiences. Not for the first time or the last, are there more than one possible answer to a given question.

The teaching is that those who would learn should sit at the feet of the Wise men who first taught the lesson, "Trust in God and seek refuge with Him".

Verse 9 is wonderfully dismissive of the good things of this world, concluding that possessions or great riches are but a passing phase, which anticipates much of the teaching of Jesus about riches.

Psalm 63. God is my help and my salvation.

Book	II
Number of verses	11
Key verse	1

Type of psalm	Lament with thanksgiving
Possible original usage and setting	Affirming God in the Liturgy of the Temple or synagogue
Including prayer or not	Prayer, but perhaps the final 3 verses are comment rather than prayer
Individual or Communal	Individual within a congregation
Date and author	Pre-exilic, Davidic by tradition, context and vocabulary
Subsequent and Contemporary significance - Messianic indications	This hymn has been a devotional foundation for millions over thousands of years!

The psalm divides easily into five sections: v. 1 longing for God at a distance; v.2-5 remembering God in the sanctuary; v.6-8 remembering God at night; v.9–10 revenge by God on persecutors and v.11 the king's faith affirmed.

The language is consistent with a pre-exilic date and the references to 'sanctuary' and not 'Temple' reinforce Davidic authorship. David may have been fleeing from Absalom (he was already king) - see 2 Kings 15.22f.

The psalm resounds with conviction, devotion and the praise of God.

Psalm 63 can be usefully compared with Psalm 23. Both are devotional classics and have been foundations upon which many have built their devotional reading.

Psalms 61, 62 and 63 all employ the metaphor of 'rock'.

Psalm 64. Let the righteous rejoice in the Lord.

Book	II
Number of verses	10
Key verse	10

Type of psalm	Lament
Possible original usage and setting	A dissertation on the sins of the wicked and their ultimate defeat. Possibly at public worship.
Including prayer or not	Prayer and narrative
Individual or Communal	Communal
Date and author	Date and author unknown other than in the superscription.
Subsequent and Contemporary significance - Messianic indications	God will ensure the welfare of the righteous in the end.

This psalm begins on a very singular note and ends with a much more comprehensive vein. "Hear my voice" is the opening, whereas, "Let all the upright in heart rejoice in the Lord" is the conclusion. The psalm develops the bitter conflict between the righteous and the wicked. All people will know by God's success that he is the Almighty One.

Psalm 64 marks the end of a long sequence of laments of different kinds from Psalm 51-64.

Psalm 65. Harvest thanksgiving.

Book	II
Number of verses	13
Key verse	9

Type of psalm	Praise with thanksgiving
Possible original usage and setting	Possibly used at the annual harvest occasions e.g. the Feast of Tabernacles or the Feast of Unleavened Bread.
Including prayer or not	Prayer and praise
Individual or Communal	Communal
Date and author	Possibly late pre-exilic
Subsequent and Contemporary significance - Messianic indications	Then and even to the present day this is the farmers' Harvest Psalm. For Christians, there are messianic overtones

Psalm 65 celebrates God as the Lord of the Harvest. God provides the rain to give growth. God is Lord of creation, and of salvation, and is the One who sustains his people. The pictures of the abundant harvest have stirred the hearts and voices of the faithful for countless generations. Such a hymn can also be interpreted messianically – the God who provides for today also prepares for tomorrow and with the realisation the worshippers singing the psalm are pointed forwards into the future. Those who gather the harvest are urged to look to the One who will end all suffering and want.

In years of intense suffering and falling rainfall figures over much of sub-Saharan Africa, could we legitimately call this Africa's special psalm?

Psalm 66. Come and see what the Lord has done.

Book	II
Number of verses	20
Key verse	16

Type of psalm	Praise
Possible original usage and setting	Temple worship, v.1–12 in the liturgy
Including prayer or not	Prayer
Individual or Communal	Communal but v.13-19 individual
Date and author	Post-exilic, author anonymous
Subsequent and Contemporary significance - Messianic indications	The Exodus after the enslavement in Egypt features largely. This can be interpreted messianically by Christians.

In verses 3 and 5, the Hebrew word *'yare'* occurs and this has a whole range of English equivalents as seen by the choices made by the different Bible translations; NEB 'fearful and tremendous'; NIV 'awesome'; RSV 'terrible'; JB 'dread and fear'; GNB 'wonderful' and Authorised Version 'terrible'. This variety of translations allows the reader to be aware of the many versions available, all of which are freely available online.

The impact of the Exodus experience upon the nation of Israel is illustrated powerfully in Psalm 66. To this very day even the modern secular state of Israel looks back to that exodus and wilderness experience with awe, and gratitude to God, and a great determination that each successive generation will know the story of their nation's past.

The final section of the psalm seems distinct and different. It becomes an individual experience and the record of that individual's piety. At the level of just one person his religious experience is then recounted.

Psalm 67. Let all the peoples praise thee.

Book	II
Number of verses	7
Key verse	1

Type of psalm	Praise
Possible original usage and setting	At Feast of Tabernacles celebration
Including prayer or not	Prayer
Individual or Communal	Communal and congregational
Date and author	Post-exilic or late pre-exilic; author anonymous
Subsequent and Contemporary significance - Messianic indications	This short psalm like Psalm 65 was a harvest celebration and thanksgiving song then and still is today.

Some translations render v. 6 in the past, and others in the future. The significance of this is that if the future tense is selected (e.g. the NIV) then the meaning is a national lament and perhaps a prayer for rain or other necessary conditions. Whereas if the past tense is chosen as the preferred translation (e.g. the AV or RSV) then the psalm becomes a hymn of praise and thanksgiving. The psalm reads like a statement of faith or belief, it is a CREDO (meaning 'I believe'). It has a similar sound to the Aaronic Blessing in Numbers 6, 24-26 and to Deuteronomy 26.1-11.

No doubt both thanksgiving for the past, and prayers for the future for continued blessings, are both parts of the believer's proper responses to God's love and goodness.

Psalm 68. A song of triumph.

Book	II
Number of verses	35
Key verses	18&20

Type of psalm	Praise
Possible original usage and setting	Liturgical hymn perhaps recited at the autumnal Feast of Weeks to celebrate God's blessings
Including prayer or not	Mainly prayer, with occasional verses addressed to the people, e.g. v. 4, or other people's e.g. v. 32
Individual or Communal	Communal for congregational worship
Date and author	Early pre-exilic, perhaps in the reign of Solomon as the Temple is mentioned in v. 29 and had not been built in David's time.
Subsequent and Contemporary significance - Messianic indications	For Christians, this has become a Pentecostal Hymn with a clear messianic message and is a comprehensive statement of Old Testament religion.

This psalm is a major statement of faith. It has been termed a story of salvation. The psalm (v. 18) is referred to in the New Testament, in Ephesian 4.8 and in Acts 2.23 (and is also quoted in Handel's Messiah e.g. v. 18). For Christians, the psalm looks forward to Christ's coming in power and is therefore often sung on Whit Sunday.

The psalm can also helpfully be called a hymn of deliverance, and it has been suggested that the whole work may originally have been more than one entity.

It is not an easy psalm to fully comprehend but it is a wonderful comprehensive examination of God's work and purposes.

Psalm 69. A cry of distress.

Book	II
Number of verses	36
Key verses	17&18

Type of psalm	Lament
Possible original usage and setting	A needy man seeking solace
Including prayer or not	Prayer except for v.30-36
Individual or Communal	Individual
Date and author	Post-exilic, perhaps sixth century BC
Subsequent and Contemporary significance - Messianic indications	Can be personally applied in any generation. This is the human condition of the needy. This great psalm can be everyman's experience at some time

Psalm 69 is a hugely penitent prayer of confession. It is a plea for forgiveness and restoration. We are not told whether the suppliant suffered illness or trauma, v. 6-7 is one of the most poignant of these prayers.

This is probably the most quoted psalm in the New Testament. Verses 4, 9, 21, 22-25, and 28 are all quoted a total of 16 times. Handel's Messiah quotes Psalm 69.20 and there are 11 other quotations from the Psalms in the text of the Messiah.

Although this psalm was perhaps first written down in the sixth century BC, the constituent prayers from which it is compiled are as old and as modern as any of us in any age can bear witness.

In verse 21 the words 'vinegar for my thirst' were echoed by Jesus on the cross and reordered in Matthew 27.34. In this psalm, Old and New Testaments are very close to one another.

Psalm 70. A prayer for help.

Book	II
Number of verses	5
Key verse	3

Type of psalm	Lament
Possible original usage and setting	Probably used in Temple worship
Including prayer or not	Prayer
Individual or Communal	Individual reference within a congregation
Date and author	Post-exilic, author anonymous
Subsequent and Contemporary significance - Messianic indications	This psalm is a doublet of Psalm 40.13-17 and may well share a common source with Psalm 40. This psalm also fits well in Christian praise.

Psalm 70 continues in the same vein as Psalm 69. Sin has been confessed, and both forgiveness and help are sought from God. v. 2 and 3 may well be sub-Christian in their theology and message, yet this is the way even Christians frequently behave in their lesser moments. There is realism in these words that commend the psalm to many who struggle to live as they ought. This is a real human being who struggled then, as women and men still struggle.

The phrase, "O Lord make haste to help me" will have been on the mind if not on the lips of all who have ever read this psalm and recall it in an hour of need.

Psalm 71. Prayer in old age.

Book	II
Number of verses	24
Key verses	9&18

Type of psalm	Lament
Possible original usage and setting	An old man's lament as he proclaims God's might to all generations.
Including prayer or not	Prayer woven into the narrative
Individual or Communal	One individual speaking, perhaps, for others
Date and author	Post-exilic, with superscription, an orphan psalm
Subsequent and Contemporary significance - Messianic indications	Psalm 71 can be read as foreshadowing Christian outreach and evangelism

The lovely story of an old man who has spent his life faithfully telling of God's mercy, majesty and power throughout his long life. God has been rock, hope, refuge and much more to this old man. The phrase 'make haste to help me' occurs both in v. 12 as it did in v. 1 of Psalm 70. These two psalms, along with Psalm 40, may well have had a common source.

It is widely taught and accepted that there is little expectation of a personal life after death indicated in any part of the Old Testament. However, in this psalm (v. 20-21) and in occasional verses in some other psalms, and occasionally elsewhere, there are indications that some at least had personal expectations beyond the grave.

This is not the best ordered psalm in the Psalter but then not uncommonly old men do sometimes get things a bit out of sequence!

Psalm 72. Prayer for the king.

Book	II
Number of verses	19
Key verses	12&13

Type of psalm	Royal psalm
Possible original usage and setting	At the enthronement of a new king or on the anniversary of an existing king in the Temple
Including prayer or not	Prayer
Individual or Communal	The congregation interceding for the king
Date and author	Pre-exilic, Solomon's name is linked with this psalm
Subsequent and Contemporary significance - Messianic indications	The early Christian Church will have interpreted this psalm messianically and the Jew may still do so.

Note: Verse 29 is a doxology to Book II.

Psalm 72 is a Royal Psalm about an earthly king but the psalmist leaves us in no doubt that God is the leading personage in these verses. God is behind and before and above and underneath, enabling the king to be His king. The extravagant claims made for the king are only possible because he the king, is enabled by God i.e. God's sovereignty, supremacy and success are achieved through the king, His agent.

This psalm crucially sets out the right relationship between God and his temporal agent-on-earth. No other ancient people were so clear about this distinction between God, king and people.

The psalm directs the king to care for the poor and the needy and the repetition of this message in v. 12 and 13 after already introducing the subject in v. 4 only serves to emphasise the centrality of this message.

Psalm 73. A true assessment of life.

Book	III
Number of verses	28
Key verses	16 & 17

Type of psalm	Wisdom. There are eleven of these, the other ten are: 1, 32, 37, 49, 78, 112, 119, 127, 128 and 133.
Possible original usage and setting	Perhaps as a cultic song as well as for educational purposes
Including prayer or not	Prayer and wisdom
Individual or Communal	For the benefit of all although arising from one man's experience.
Date and author	Post-exilic by an anonymous Wise man
Subsequent and Contemporary significance - Messianic indications	The problem of undeserved suffering, theodicy, remains to this day

Wisdom teaches that the righteous will prosper and be safe. However, the opposite is not true - suffering does not mean that the sufferer has necessarily deserved his suffering. So, although this is not a Christian belief it is of course widely accepted and followed.

Psalm 73 is typical 'wisdom speak'. This same vocabulary is to be found in Proverbs, Job and Ecclesiastes. The problem facing the psalmist here is almost identical to Job's problem (in the Book by that name). The psalm stops short of teaching that if you are wealthy nothing can harm you!

Jesus of course repudiates this in the parable of the rich young ruler, "Go sell all that you have and follow me." (Matthew 19.21)

For many, Psalm 73.21-23 are the core of the song and represent the way forward.

Psalm 74. In a time of national humiliation.

Book	III
Number of verses	23
Key verse	3

Type of psalm	Lament
Possible original usage and setting	To encourage a return to God
Including prayer or not	Prayer included
Individual or Communal	Communal
Date and author	Exilic or post-exilic written by an anonymous priest or a prophet, possibly just after the exile.
Subsequent and Contemporary significance - Messianic indications	Israel was again calling upon God to restore her fortunes as she has had to do so very often.

Verses 1-11 along with v.22-23 seem to outline one real situation, but verses 12-21 seem to reflect a different situation. In the case of the former this seems to reflect a low ebb in Israel's fortunes.

This psalm is difficult to interpret. Questions arise: Is the Temple in use or not? Does the psalm refer to the Babylonian destruction in 587 BC or to the Antiochus Epiphanes' destruction much later in 167 BC? Or is it possible that the psalm refers to the hypothetical pollution of the Temple under Artaxerxes in the fourth century BC? This is a dramatic psalm which is difficult to locate to a particular time.

Verse 8 is translated as 'synagogue' in the Authorised Version whereas the RSV refers to 'meeting places', and the New English Bible to 'God's holy places'. The NIV renders v. 8, "They burned every place where God was worshipped in the land".

These examples illustrate how difficult it is to be either precise or dogmatic about the history or meaning of Psalm 74.

Psalm 75. God is judge.

Book	III
Number of verses	10
Key verse	5

Type of psalm	Praise with thanksgiving
Possible original usage and setting	A prophetic liturgy – God in dialogue with a person or a congregation
Including prayer or not	Prayer
Individual or Communal	Communal
Date and author	Exilic or post–exilic by possibly a cultic prophet
Subsequent and Contemporary significance - Messianic indications	Here the community give thanks, and God through a prophet responds

Verse 5 may hold a key to the meaning, "Do not lift up your *horn*". Horn here is controversial usage. Horn is a composite word expressing something like strength, might, pride and dignity. There seems to be no single word expressing 'horn'. Maybe a phrase such as 'Don't get ideas above your station' or simply, 'who do you think you are?'

In the end, it is God Himself who promotes or elevates one person and relegates another in terms of real status. 1 Samuel 2.1ff expresses the same truth. God's promotion is effected and Hannah's prayer is answered. This psalm indeed teaches that God is the chief arbitrator. In this relatively simple psalm the teaching establishes the significance of God and his subjects. This is a crucial directive for all would be believers!

Psalm 76. God triumphant.

Book	III
Number of verses	12
Key verse	3

Type of psalm	Praise
Possible original usage and setting	Temple for the Feast of Tabernacles is a possibility
Including prayer or not	Verses 4-12 are addressed to God.
Individual or Communal	Communal, the worship of the congregation
Date and author	Pre-exilic and later adopted for Temple use
Subsequent and Contemporary significance - Messianic indications	Can be read as a powerful anti-war hymn

A four-fold division is appropriate: v. 1-3 God magnified; v. 4-6 God's victory; v. 7-9 the power of the Divine Judge is supreme and v. 10-12 our need to praise God. However, critics are not unanimous and there are other possible divisions. It is difficult so long after the event to connect this psalm to a particular historical situation but it is possible that it looks back to the time before Israel and Judah were separate kingdoms. The use of the terms Judah and Israel in v.1 emphasises this.

The psalm may now legitimately be read and heard as a strong anti-war hymn which highlights the futility of conflict and ascribes all real power to God. The power, might and majesty of God are contrasted to inability of men of war to use either their hands or their weapons.

Psalm 77. Meditations on days gone by.

Book	III
Number of verses	20
Key verse	13

Type of psalm	Lament which gives way to praise from v. 11
Possible original usage and setting	Meditations by an individual, perhaps culled from older cultic traditions
Including prayer or not	More a talk with God
Individual or Communal	Individual musings
Date and author	Pre-exilic possibly, anonymous
Subsequent and Contemporary significance - Messianic indications	For all people, everywhere there is the oscillating assessment of God's presence and power

The material comprising Psalm 77 appears to be arranged in a cyclic form. Verse 1 is positive and then the psalm spirals downwards into the depths of despair (v. 9-10) and then finally recovers again to a position of renewed faith. This pattern is followed in a number of psalms.

But the meaning and the message of the psalm are not at all obvious. It has been suggested that v. 1-9, 10 -15, and 16 – 20 were originally from three separate older sources.

This may or may not be true, and, rather than ponder the imponderable, it is perhaps more profitable to accept the psalm as it is, and realise it is a journey that each one can make as they read. The mood goes from the positive right down to the depths of despair but then rises again with an increased grasp and an improved understanding of God's saving power.

Psalm 78. Lessons from Israel's history.

Book	III
Number of verses	72
Key verse	4

Type of psalm	Wisdom, the sixth of the eleven Wisdom psalms. See psalm 1 for the full list.
Possible original usage and setting	Perhaps used at worship during Festivals, in order to remember and recite the nation's history
Including prayer or not	More a lesson than a prayer
Individual or Communal	Communal
Date and author	Probably late pre-exilic, anonymous
Subsequent and Contemporary significance - Messianic indications	Psalm 78.2 is quoted by Jesus in Matthew 13,35 and Psalm 78.24 is quoted in John 6.31,32 and Psalm 78.18 in Matthew 4.3

The prophets, the priests and the wise men all delighted in telling and re-telling the story or history of Israel time and time again. Psalm 78 is one such telling. The sequence spelled out in v. 32–35 is repeated many times in the Old Testament; that sequence is sin is followed by punishment, punishment by repentance, repentance by restoration and restoration leading to more sin!

Jewish parents in every generation have set great store by the telling of the faith stories by the old to the succeeding generations. The process continues to this day. Psalm 78 tells the story from the Exodus from Egypt to the reign of King David (approx. tenth century BC). So, the psalm is both history lesson and instruction on how to live and behave in both national and personal matters. This is wisdom teaching woven together with history lessons.

This is one of longest psalms. Others are 89,106 and 119.

Psalm 79. Lament over the destruction of Jerusalem.

Book	III
Number of verses	13
Key verse	5

Type of psalm	Lament
Possible original usage and setting	The language of liturgy and the worship in either Temple or synagogue
Including prayer or not	Prayer
Individual or Communal	Communal
Date and author	Possibly during the exile, author unknown
Subsequent and Contemporary significance - Messianic indications	Even in exile, the Jews retained their national identity and still do to this very day.

The psalm appears to depict the devastation, destruction and dereliction of Jerusalem inflicted by Babylon upon Jerusalem and Judah in 586 BC, developing further the theme of Psalm 78. There is huge sadness in these words and they reflect a National Disaster (Compare Psalms 44 and 74).

The people's lament is in v. 1–4 and the prayers of the remnant are in v. 5-12. Finally, in v. 13 there is an expression of hope and confidence.

Whether this was written in Babylon or among the ruins in Jerusalem is difficult to say. Certainly, sadness is the keynote.

Verse 5 remains one of the gloomiest verses in the Old Testament. A question asked by the Jews down through their history, in this instance asking how long before Jerusalem would be restored, later asking when would Israel return, and always asking when would the Messiah come. And of course, Jews still ask the question.

Psalm 80. O Lord of hosts restore us!

Book	III
Number of verses	19
Key verses	3,7, &19

Type of psalm	Lament
Possible original usage and setting	Temple liturgy, prayers for restoration and return
Including prayer or not	Prayer – fervent!
Individual or Communal	Communal
Date and author	Perhaps immediately post-exilic, author anonymous
Subsequent and Contemporary significance - Messianic indications	Compare Psalm 80.8 with Isaiah 5.1ff, this can be a Messianic psalm for Jew and for Christian. Looking forward to that which is not yet.

Two images are used: that of the shepherd in v. 1 ff. and of the vine in v. 8 ff. God is the shepherd of Israel, and Israel is likened to a vine. Both these images occur elsewhere in the Old and New Testaments.

The disaster that has befallen Israel is either that of Israel in 722 BC, at the hands of the Assyrians, or 586 BC when Judah fell to the Babylonians. Alternatively, this could be set in the seventh century BC in the time of King Josiah.

Thus, the chapter is a seminar in Israel's sacred history and serves to underline the intimate relationship between Israel and their God.

The fervent prayer is given added emphasis in the thrice repeated refrain, "*Restore us O God of hosts... let thy face shine that we may be saved*".

Psalm 81. God calls Israel to obedience.

Book	III
Number of verses	15
Key verse	10

Type of psalm	Praise
Possible original usage and setting	Possibly used at the Feast of Tabernacles to exhort Israel to obedience
Including prayer or not	Not prayer but rather the priest or prophet speaking, as it were, for God to the people.
Individual or Communal	Communal
Date and author	Post-exilic, author anonymous
Subsequent and Contemporary significance - Messianic indications	Restoration is a Messianic theme and so for both Jews and early Christians this could have highlighted the importance of Psalm 81.

Here the divine voice declares divine truths, and some of the miracles of God's intervention are set down (Compare Ps 95). These intrusions on Israel's behalf have determined Israel's subsequent history from Egypt to Palestine to Babylon and back again.

The Feast of Tabernacles seems to accord best with the timetable suggested in v. 3. The whole range of musical devices is enlightening and may indicate that percussion, string, and wind instruments were all used in Temple worship in ancient Israel.

The idea that a Temple official would speak for God is a fascinating idea giving us a glimpse of how vibrant and vital their worship will have been.

Psalm 82. God's judgment on false gods.

Book	III
Number of verses	8
Key verse	8

Type of psalm	Praise
Possible original usage and setting	Temple liturgy. A plea for restoration
Including prayer or not	Probably not a prayer
Individual or Communal	Communal expression or dialogue with God
Date and author	Post-exilic psalm by an unknown Temple official
Subsequent and Contemporary significance - Messianic indications	That was and this still is a confusing world to live in!

The crucial question in seeking to understand this psalm is to identify the "gods". There are several possibilities: they can be compared to the divine assembly mentioned in the Book of Job, chapters 1 and 2, or they are Israel's corrupt judges, or they have been compared to the gods of other nations. Clearly Jesus is referring to these same "gods" in John 10.34.

What the author of this psalm longs for is for God to judge the earth with equity, and to make good his claim to be the God of the entire world and all the nations. Only in that way will there be justice. The identity of the "gods" will doubtless continue to be debated but the right and the need for our God to judge the nations with equity remains an imperative.

Psalm 82 is a reminder and a caution – we will never understand fully the message and the meaning of all the psalms!

Psalm 83. Prayer during a national crisis.

Book	III
Number of verses	18
Key verse	18

Type of psalm	Lament
Possible original usage and setting	Used as a national lament at an undefined time of disaster
Including prayer or not	Prayer
Individual or Communal	Communal for the nation
Date and author	Post exilic, perhaps a Temple official or musician
Subsequent and Contemporary significance - Messianic indications	In spite of the angst, aggression and sadness of the nation then, and often since, nations look to God.

In Psalm 83 the psalmist petitions God to annihilate Israel's enemies! He identifies those wicked people who have plotted against Israel and has designated them as God's enemies. The psalmist suggests dreadful punishments and misfortunes for them.

This is perhaps the most extreme 'cursing psalm' (compare 2 Chronicles 20) and yet, in spite of all the anger and bitterness, the psalmist wants people to know that Israel's God is the Lord of all the earth (v. 18).

The psalmist wants God to eliminate all Israel's enemies. This is difficult for Christians, not so much for the sentiment expressed but for the totality. It is somehow not appropriate for God to be asked to behave in such a way although this will be how people feel. So, the cursing psalms raise all sorts of dilemmas and crises of conscience.

Psalm 84. How lovely is thy dwelling place?

Book	III
Number of verses	12
Key verse	10

Type of psalm	Praise
Possible original usage and setting	Most likely at the Annual Feast of Tabernacles in the Temple
Including prayer or not	Prayer
Individual or Communal	Individual with a wide reference
Date and author	Pre-exilic, confirmed by the reference to a king, author likely to be a Temple servant
Subsequent and Contemporary significance - Messianic indications	Psalm 84 has been praise in every age, and longing in every believer's heart for the Father's house

Zion has several meanings including a mountain near Jerusalem, and a term for God's house or heaven. The psalm expresses a prayer that life's desired end is in God's company. This Old Testament prayer converts easily into a Christian prayer and renders Psalm 84 a strongly Messianic hymn.

Thus, the traveller, and this is a traveller's psalm, prays that he may live every day with God and underlying the daily prayer is the dream, the vision, the passionate desire to be eternally in God's presence in what is called heaven. This is not only a hymn for Bunyan's Pilgrim to sing, but the hymn for all pilgrims to sing as they walk life's rocky way (this psalm has similarities to the Songs of Ascent Psalms 120-134).

Psalm 85. A prayer for peace.

Book	III
Number of verses	13
Key verse	8

Type of psalm	Lament
Possible original usage and setting	Temple worship to express trust in the Lord
Including prayer or not	Prayer
Individual or Communal	Communal
Date and author	Post-exilic, anonymous, perhaps a Temple priest
Subsequent and Contemporary significance - Messianic indications	A prayer for peace is always appropriate in a war-torn world

Psalm 85 may be the records of what happened after the return from Babylon in c. 560 BC. The psalm divides up as: v. 1-3 return from Babylon; v. 4-7 the distress from which relief was sought and v. 8-13 (or at least 10-13). The climax of the psalm is, according to Derek Kidner (1973), "One of the most satisfying descriptions of concord, both spiritual and material to be found anywhere in scripture." Pg. 308.

Thus, the sequence of the psalm is from lament, to relief with thanksgiving. While this interpretation is reasonable it may well not be the only reasonable way to understand this very moving testimony. There are real similarities between this psalm and Psalm 126, one of the Psalms of Ascent. The lament is imbued with the sense that God will always protect.

Psalm 86. The prayer of a needy man.

Book	III
Number of verses	17
Key verse	15

Type of psalm	Lament but also involving praise and royalty.
Possible original usage and setting	In worship, or in a procession
Including prayer or not	Prayer
Individual or Communal	Individual, a penitent king is possible
Date and author	Pre-exilic, and David as a possible author
Subsequent and Contemporary significance - Messianic indications	The sentiments are those in any age seeking God's favour. Psalm 86 remains a pattern for approaching God in prayer

Who can pray such a prayer? Probably no mere human being can reach this level of penitence and subservience. The self-righteousness of the supplicant in v. 2 is embarrassing to read and therefore it is difficult to identify these words with any ordinary sinful human being, past or present, even King David. Therefore, it is by understanding this psalm as being messianic in intent, and pointing forwards to one who is to come, that it is possible to come to some appreciation and understanding of this difficult lament.

For Christians, it is probably only by putting the words upon the lips of Jesus that it is possible to receive it and read it as if it were from the lips of Jesus. There are also other psalms in this same category e.g. Psalm 26. This psalm looks forward to such a One who is to come.

Psalm 87. Glorious things of thee are spoken.

Book	III
Number of verses	7
Key verse	3

Type of psalm	Praise
Possible original usage and setting	Use in worship in a dance procession – see v. 7
Including prayer or not	Not prayer but praise
Individual or Communal	Communal
Date and author	Either exilic or post-exilic, anonymous
Subsequent and Contemporary significance - Messianic indications	This short hymn reveals great affection for Jerusalem and from that an eschatological and messianic understanding is implied.

Psalm 87 has made its way into Christian praise through John Newton's eighteenth-century hymn "Glorious things of thee are spoken, Zion city of our God". The identity of the speaker is obscure, and this appears almost to be a psalm about predestination!

The psalm may also be the origin of the phrase in Galatians 4.26, "The Jerusalem above is our mother".

This psalm is one of a sub-group of Praise Psalms which can be entitled Hymns of Zion and include Psalms 46, 48, 76, 84, and 122. The question has been asked as to whether this psalm is a finished work or the incomplete fragment of a lost original? It is difficult if not impossible to answer such questions. There appear to be three meanings for Zion – Jerusalem, or where God lives, or the eternal city. Only the context determines the choice. There are more unanswered questions than answers about Psalm 87.

Psalm 88. Face to face with death.

Book	III
Number of verses	18
Key verse	3

Type of psalm	Lament
Possible original usage and setting	In the Temple, or in the synagogue, a distressed suppliant seeks help
Including prayer or not	Prayer
Individual or Communal	Individual
Date and author	Post-exilic, unknown author
Subsequent and Contemporary significance - Messianic indications	The problem of theodicy, undeserved suffering (with which Job wrestled), is presented here.

A tragic tale of a very sorry man! Some say this is the Psalter's saddest psalm. Traditionally read in Christian churches at Good Friday services. The New Century Bible speaks of unrelieved gloom, perhaps suggesting that there may have been a lost ending which was more positive. The psalm is reminiscent not only of Job but also of Jeremiah, the Book of Lamentations and of parts of Bunyan's Pilgrim's Progress (Bunyan 1678). Or at a more mundane level perhaps this psalm is the experience of everyone at some time in their life.

The inability to realise the presence of God, when he is deaf to every call, when prayer seems to be words into a vacuum, seems to be an integral part of the dialogue of faith, part of the pilgrim's anguish. Therefore, such a psalm has to be present in the Psalter so that even the loneliest pilgrim knows a travelling companion!

Psalm 89. God's covenant with David.

Book	III
Number of verses	51
Key verse	11

Type of psalm	Royal Psalm, seventh of eleven, Psalms 2, 18, 20, 21, 45, 72, 89, 101, 110, 132 and 144 or, a Mixed type
Possible original usage and setting	Many different uses and settings have been suggested
Including prayer or not	In part prayer, v. 46ff.
Individual or Communal	Communal
Date and author	Post-exilic, author unknown
Subsequent and Contemporary significance - Messianic indications	A difficult psalm to relate chronologically, although the emphasis on the Davidic line suggests a messianic interpretation for Christians

The psalm divides into: v.1- 18 hymn; v. 19-37 reviewing David's covenant; v.38-45 lament; and v. 46-51 prayer. Psalm 89 is believed to have been based on 2 Samuel 7.4-7.

The tension is presented between God's enduring love and the harsh reality of misfortune, defeat and trouble. The first part is a reflection on Israel and David's dynasty, and on creation and the covenant relationship. The psalm is about the King of kings and David his regent. One of the basics is that God's love will never leave David and the Davidic line. There is the continual contrast between God's extravagant providing and the harsh reality of life in war and strife torn Judah.

Note: There is a doxology, v.52, concluding Book III.

Psalm 90. From everlasting to everlasting you are God.

Book	IV
Number of verses	17
Key verse	12

Type of psalm	Lament
Possible original usage and setting	In the Temple at penitential services within the liturgy
Including prayer or not	Prayer
Individual or Communal	Communal
Date and author	Post-exilic, although some accept Moses as author
Subsequent and Contemporary significance - Messianic indications	For Christians, this is a psalm that will often be used at funerals, speaking as it does of the brevity of human life.

Psalm 90, which is at the beginning of Book IV, is a powerful opening. Isaiah 40 and Psalm 90 together present the grandeur of God in unsurpassed adoration. This is a psalm of contrasts, between the eternity of God and the shortness and little consequence of human life. The superscription associating the psalm with Moses is the only one to do so.

A further mark of the uniqueness of Psalm 90 is that it uses both Yahweh and Elohim as words for God. This comes out very clearly in the Jerusalem Bible. Although the psalm is a lament there are also wisdom words such as v. 12. Verse 15 is both evocative and comforting as well as being a chilly reminder of life's uncertainties.

In all of this the plea in the final verse that God would recognise our significance is very moving. Which one of us does not yearn for a little significance?

Psalm 91. Living with the Lord.

Book	IV
Number of verses	16
Key verse	11

Type of psalm	Praise
Possible original usage and setting	Both liturgical perhaps to accompany a grand entrance to the Temple, and for teaching.
Including prayer or not	Both a prayer and some of God's answers to prayer
Individual or Communal	Communal, and also appropriate for any seeking servant.
Date and author	Both anonymous and timeless, probably post-exilic
Subsequent and Contemporary significance - Messianic indications	Psalm 91 is quoted in the account of the temptations of Jesus in both Matthew and Luke's Gospels, and still quoted often!

This wonderful hymn expresses the protection and the security that God offers those who love Him and seek to serve Him. Here are words for the largest gathering or the most intimate personal and private prayer. This psalm is a measure of the love of God for all who turn to Him. Henri Nouven (1994), in his "The return of the Prodigal Son," makes this comment on Psalm 91.1-4, "And so, under the aspect of an old Jewish patriarch, there emerges also a motherly God receiving her son home." pg. 100. The psalm speaks not only of God's protection for the individual but for the whole community. The references to this psalm in the Gospels is good evidence that in the first century AD the psalm was well-known and was quoted to illustrate God's love for the individual.

C.S. Lewis (1958) suggests that these must be the very words Jesus spoke since only He could be the source of the temptation story (v. 11-12).

Psalm 92. Praise to the Most High.

Book	IV
Number of verses	15
Key verse	1

Type of psalm	Praise with thanksgiving and using some "wisdom" vocabulary. A Mixed type psalm
Possible original usage and setting	In the liturgy, by the congregation, for the praise of God
Including prayer or not	Prayer from verse 8
Individual or Communal	Communal and individual see especially verse 10f
Date and author	Post exilic, author unknown
Subsequent and Contemporary significance - Messianic indications	Some Christian hymns follow this pattern, e.g.by Isaac Watts and others.

The mood of the psalm changes radically from the uninhibited praise of v. 1- 5 and 12 -15 to the near vitriol of v.6–11. C.S. Lewis (1958) comments that the 'evil' words are those we might not express but nevertheless think! It is not good to take satisfaction from the misfortune of others, such words as these can trouble many psalm reading Christians.

Derek Kidner (1973), in his Tyndale Commentary, sees this psalm as particularly appropriate for Sunday worship, picking up on the superscription that Psalm 92 is for the Sabbath day. This is an indication that the superscription was added much later.

Here is praise that seems equally applicable and appropriate for both individuals and congregations.

Psalm 93. God, you are forever.

Book	IV
Number of verses	5
Key verse	2

Type of psalm	Praise
Possible original usage and setting	Possibly an Enthronement hymn, or sung at the Feast of Tabernacles
Including prayer or not	Prayer (v. 2, 5) and Hymn (v. 1, 3, 4)
Individual or Communal	Communal
Date and author	Post-exilic
Subsequent and Contemporary significance - Messianic indications	There is a timeless content in this psalm – it is in part eschatological – to do with last things.

Psalms 93-99 and possibly 100 may all be hymns written to celebrate God's annual enthronement occasion and also used at the Feast of Tabernacles to celebrate God's rule. The theme is His everlasting rule and kingship. Therefore, although Psalms 93–100 are not Royal Psalms as such, they are all to do with God's rule on earth, suggesting this prayer:

Lord the mystery of your majesty is all around and beyond
Your reign stretches back to the very beginning
You as Holy Spirit are present even now
The future of eternity is with you,
Lord you are stronger than the mightiest wave and your way is sure
And your son Jesus Christ revealed to us that He is the Way the Truth and the Life
Amen
(Gordon R 2003 pg. 23).

Psalm 94. Judge over all the earth.

Book	IV
Number of verses	23
Key verse	12

Type of psalm	Lament
Possible original usage and setting	For teaching
Including prayer or not	Includes prayer, but also address to friends and enemies
Individual or Communal	Communal
Date and author	Late post-exilic, psalmist could be a priest or a prophet or a wise man.
Subsequent and Contemporary significance - Messianic indications	A psalm that is probably little known and little used! One of the difficult 'cursing psalms'

The difficult choices are to decide who is addressing whom: v. 1–7 psalmist to God; v. 8–11 psalmist speaks to senseless ones; v. 12–15 psalmist prays; v. 16–19 psalmist to congregation of the faithful and v. 20–23 psalmist ponders his dilemma. The psalm declares that God will destroy bad people and bad rulers. This is a sad psalm full of regrets and desire for revenge. Indeed, this also qualifies to be one of the 'cursing' psalms where the psalmist resorts to what we consider inappropriate responses for a holy man. The sheer complexity of the relationships and one of the few clear lines emerging is that wicked rulers cannot be allied with God.

This remains one of the few psalms where it is difficult to identify an appropriate situation for it to be sung, recited or chanted.

Psalm 95. Come let us sing to the Lord.

Book	IV
Number of verses	11
Key verse	1

Type of psalm	Praise
Possible original usage and setting	In the Temple liturgy, possibly at the Feast of Tabernacles, or enthronement occasion
Including prayer or not	Not prayer
Individual or Communal	Communal
Date and author	Pre-exilic, some say by King David
Subsequent and Contemporary significance - Messianic indications	Popular over many centuries in Christian churches sung as "O Come and let us to the Lord", the Venite.

When a psalm has two fragments as here, with the first 7 verses a straightforward hymn and the second fragment from v. 8 appears to be a proclamation from a priest or a prophet declaring God's instructions to his people, then some will say this has originally been two psalms. However, others will maintain its unity as prophetic liturgy. Certainly, in many hymn books this one psalm has given rise to several distinct different hymns!

The metrical version of Psalm 95 has been a popular psalm, with or without accompaniment, for many years.

The metaphor of 'rock' is used here and in other psalms. Clearly this frequent use of the term led to its being taken up in the New Testament, and used of Peter by Christ himself, "You are the rock and upon you...".

A further New Testament link is the use in Hebrews 3.7-11 and 4.3-11 of the passage Psalm 95.7-11.

Psalm 96. O sing a new song to the Lord.

Book	IV
Number of verses	13
Key verse	1

Type of psalm	Praise
Possible original usage and setting	As with Psalm 95, this psalm may originally have been used for in the Temple for the annual enthronement occasion
Including prayer or not	Not a prayer
Individual or Communal	Communal
Date and author	Difficult to be dogmatic, King David unlikely say the majority of scholars
Subsequent and Contemporary significance - Messianic indications	Reminiscent of Psalm 95. These two are a pair of similar praises, which are very popular Christian praise.

Psalms 95 and 96 are very similar. Psalm 96 is particularly about judgement. Many Christians dread the idea and are frightened. In contrast, Jews of all centuries from pre-exilic to modern, look forward with eager longing to that great day! Many Christian see themselves as the prisoners in the dock on trial whereas Jews are the plaintiffs seeking a good outcome. C.S. Lewis (1958) points out that many Christians tremble at the thought, whereas in the psalms it is all about rejoicing. This is most explicit in the final two verses.

In the New Testament, the woman in Luke 18 wanted to get to court to hear the good decision that she knew would be in her favour. The psalms have a wonderfully redemptive understanding of God's judgement – nowhere more than in Psalm 96. Psalm 96 also occurs as 1 Chronicles 16.23-33

Psalm 97. The Lord is King!

Book	IV
Number of verses	12
Key verse	6

Type of psalm	Praise
Possible original usage and setting	Temple liturgy for celebrating God's annual enthronement
Including prayer or not	Not a prayer
Individual or Communal	Communal as Israel rejoices
Date and author	Post-exilic, author unknown
Subsequent and Contemporary significance - Messianic indications	The phrase 'light dawns for the righteous' can be interpreted messianically.

The psalm has two parts: v. 1–6 declares the majesty of Yahweh and v. 7–12 the significance of His rule. This psalm is pervaded by a spirit of prophecy, and may have developed older pre-exilic material, which is a practice of many hymn writers in every generation.

The psalmist demonstrates the rule of God by asserting God's presence, by re-telling the history of salvation, and by describing the power of creation. The reign of God makes possible new life, and this new life may be interpreted in a variety of ways – including messianically. This is illustrated in verses 11-12.

Psalm 97.7 is quoted in Hebrews 1.6.

Repeatedly through this hymn of praise the righteousness and justice of God's rule is emphasised.

Psalm 98. The Judge of all the world.

Book	IV
Number of verses	9
Key verse	4

Type of psalm	Praise
Possible original usage and setting	Liturgical use in giving thanks and praise for God's/Yahweh's deliverance.
Including prayer or not	Praise, not prayer
Individual or Communal	Communal in the congregation
Date and author	Post-exilic. Psalms 96, 97, 98 are all similar in style and content, perhaps indicating the same author
Subsequent and Contemporary significance - Messianic indications	In many ways, the model for a Christian hymn looking forward to deliverance in God's time

God's reign was the basis of the Davidic line of kings (v. 4). Psalm 98 has a long history in the Christian Church and is used to demonstrate God's reign in creation and in nature.

In response to all the activity of God the community gathers and through these   psalms articulate the praise of God and looks forward to His final deliverance.

There is much in common between Psalms 96–98 and the content of Isaiah 40-55.

This psalm has a long and honoured history in the reformed Church where in one version the following line can be found, *"O sing a new song to Jehovah for He wondrous things hath wrought"*.

Psalm 99. Our God reigns!

Book	IV
Number of verses	9
Key verse	1

Type of psalm	Praise
Possible original usage and setting	Psalms 95–99 are all possible Enthronement Psalms, and used at Feast of Tabernacles in the Temple liturgy
Including prayer or not	Praise not prayer
Individual or Communal	Communal
Date and author	Pre-exilic but not attributed to David
Subsequent and Contemporary significance - Messianic indications	"Our God reigns" will be one modern psalm developing from Psalm 99

This group of psalms from 94-99 all praise God's rule in similar words and Psalm 99 is about covenant renewal. They all celebrate Yahweh's rule and his future rule. The emphasis is on the Holiness of God, signifying God's goodness, God's greatness God's otherness and God's power. They do so in different terms but yet the cumulative effect is of awe before the Supreme Ruler. Consequently, these psalms have been a fertile ground for wonderful Christian praise and "Our God reigns" is a good example.

This psalm majors in the appropriate attitude and response from the worshippers. Trembling is fitting for the people, for even the earth will 'quake' (v. 1). This psalm spans history, encompasses the universe, and leaves the worshipper with a wonderful appreciation of the holiness of God. The Christian Church has inherited such wonderful praise from the people of Israel 3000 years ago.

Psalm 100. All people that on earth do sing!

Book	IV
Number of verses	5
Key verse	3

Type of psalm	Praise
Possible original usage and setting	Temple worship where it would be appropriate for most festivals, for praise and thanksgiving
Including prayer or not	Praise not prayer
Individual or Communal	Communal, expressing thanksgiving
Date and author	Could be pre-exilic, author unknown
Subsequent and Contemporary significance – Messianic indications	Wide Christian usage in churches great and small!

One of the best known of all the psalms in the metrical version. It is the corner stone of public worship in the Church of Scotland and many other Presbyterian churches. It is also widely sung in plain song in Episcopal Churches and in monastic Christian communities.

Psalm 100 is the final enthronement psalm - the others being 47, 93 and 95–99.

The psalm is addressed to God's people rather than to God and exhorts them all to sing the praise of their God. God is recognised as creator and sustainer and once again as so often in the prophets and the psalms God is recognised as shepherd. The 'shepherd' image is present often in both the Old and New Testaments.

At the beginning of any church service this psalm is a most powerful invitation and encouragement to worship. However, the psalm invites not only Christian believers but ALL people to join in the praise of God.

Psalm 101. The perfect ruler.

Book	IV
Number of verses	8
Key verse	1

Type of psalm	Royal psalm (8th of 11)
Possible original usage and setting	At the king's inaugural vows and each subsequent enthronement anniversary
Including prayer or not	Prayer in part, especially v.1-2
Individual or Communal	Individual
Date and author	Davidic king possibly David himself
Subsequent and Contemporary significance - Messianic indications	Can be interpreted by Christians as a messianic psalm which was looking forward to Christ's coming

This is no ordinary king making a promise to both God and to his subjects. This is a King beyond all human expectations, a King who can only be interpreted messianically, i.e. the Jews will still be waiting for such a One, and Christians will understand this hymn fulfilled in Jesus, and to be fulfilled for ever on Jesus' Second Coming.

Psalm 101 may well have been a king's annual promise to his people and perhaps King David was the first king to utter these words. This same psalm has inspired many Christian hymns like, "Blessed assurance, Jesus is mine" a nineteenth century hymn by Fanny Jane Crosby (Church Hymnary CH4 2007). This Royal psalm can be interpreted as the Messiah looking forward to His reign in His redeemed world.

Psalm 102. A Prayer for restoration.

Book	IV
Number of verses	28
Key verse	1

Type of psalm	Lament
Possible original usage and setting	Public and private, possibly at the Harvest and New Year Festivals
Including prayer or not	Prayer
Individual or Communal	Both individual and communal
Date and author	Exilic or early post-exilic
Subsequent and Contemporary significance - Messianic indications	Penitence is always appropriate. Zion (v. 13, 16 and 21) can be variously understood. Psalm 102 is recognised as one of the seven Penitential Psalms

Zion occurs with variations of meaning throughout the Psalter. It can mean Jerusalem, or it can mean God's Holy Mountain, or can be a synonym for heaven. In this psalm, the nation and an individual have problems and cause for lament. The suppliant cries to God for mercy and for acceptance (v. 1–11). In v. 12–22 the nation and the city call out for restoration, and in v.25–28 God's everlasting power and creativity are recognised.

Psalm 102.25-27 is quoted in the New Testament in the Letter to the Hebrews 1.10-12.

Two issues dominate this psalm, the penitence of the suppliant, and God's willingness to restore both the nation and the individuals comprising that nation.

Psalm 103. Bless the Lord O my soul, and heal me!

Book	IV
Number of verses	22
Key verse	13

Type of psalm	Praise
Possible original usage and setting	Individual thanksgiving may be the major usage but that does not exclude Psalm 103 from liturgical worship
Including prayer or not	Prayer and praise woven together
Individual or Communal	Individual and yet congregational
Date and author	Pre-exilic and often attributed to David
Subsequent and Contemporary significance - Messianic indications	Has been a Christian praise for countless centuries and has given rise to hymns like, "Praise my soul the king of heaven".

Psalm 103 is about what God is like and what God does. The suppliant recognises his indebtedness to God. The psalmist knows intimately a God who creates, saves, heals, protects, forgives and much more! Psalm 103 is a catalogue of good reasons to acknowledge God. It has often been heard at funerals but also at occasions expressing gratitude to God for healing. Beautifully, it is a psalm for both whispering and shouting. The psalm moves from the singular to the plural. It is a hymn expressing the gratitude of old and young, male and female, rich and poor. The psalm is thrilling in its scope and comprehensiveness.

No wonder Mary, the mother of Jesus, quotes Psalm 103 in her Magnificat in Luke 1.50. While not a specifically messianic psalm nevertheless here is yet another Old Testament / New Testament bridge.

Psalm 104. A hymn of creation.

Book	IV
Number of verses	35
Key verse	24

Type of psalm	Praise
Possible original usage and setting	A liturgical hymn for Temple use to stimulate a congregation's vision
Including prayer or not	Not prayer but praise
Individual or Communal	For both communal and personal use
Date and author	By a "Wordsworth of the ancients" New Century Bible Commentary by A.A. Anderson (1972 pg. 717)
Subsequent and Contemporary significance - Messianic indications	Still in use today for personal and congregational devotions.

Psalms 103 and 104 have much in common. Both stimulate readers to think beyond the accepted frame and to grow in their appreciation of God. Some scholars have also seen a similarity to an Egyptian Hymn to Aten. That may or may not be so but the fact remains that this psalm can be a prayer for everyone everywhere, but on a good day!

Whereas Psalm 103 was all about people, Psalm 104 concentrates more on the natural world and man only gets a brief mention in v. 15, 23 and 33-35. There is also a similarity of content between this psalm and Genesis 1.

There are four other great creation hymns in the Psalter, Psalms 8, 19, 65, and 148.

Whereas we commented in the table above that the original usage was probably in the Temple, nevertheless the psalm may have had a long oral pre-history coming from the gathered praise of many people and many groups.

Psalm 105. Israel's wonderful history.

Book	IV
Number of verses	45
Key verse	11

Type of psalm	Praise
Possible original usage and setting	Primarily for worship but also for teaching the faith presumably to the young
Including prayer or not	More propaganda than prayer
Individual or Communal	Communal
Date and author	Written post-exilically about pre-exilic times by a now unknown psalmist
Subsequent and Contemporary significance - Messianic indications	The salvation history of the Jews is also the salvation history of the Christian Church.

Whereas the previous psalm is all about the natural world this one is the historical record of how God favoured Israel above all others to establish them in Palestine. It was resisted then and still is For Christians committed to peace and reconciliation this is a difficult psalm. But as is often the case we see now only part of the picture and part of the story.

There are cross-references here to both Deuteronomy 26.1-5 and to 1 Chronicles 16.8-22, which is of course an example of a psalm occurring outside of the Psalter. The author clearly has an intimate and detailed knowledge of his people's history.

Psalm 78 recorded six of the plagues and here in Psalm 105 there are eight listed. The final chapter of the incidents recorded here are enacted in the Entry of the Ark into Jerusalem and it implies that there is more to follow.

Psalm 106. Repeated disobedience and restoration.

Book	IV
Number of verses	47
Key verse	6

Type of psalm	Lament
Possible original usage and setting	Repentance for Israel's sin in public worship
Including prayer or not	Prayer and penitence
Individual or Communal	Communal
Date and author	Early post-exilic, anonymous
Subsequent and Contemporary significance - Messianic indications	Jew and Christian are made history aware through this psalm

Psalms 78, 105 and 106 all deal with Israel's sacred history. History is presented again and again as the four-fold sequence of: sin – punishment – repentance – restoration. Israel understood their fortunes and misfortunes as God's direct action following their misdemeanours and subsequent penitence. This understanding of history is often called Deuteronomic Orthodoxy. Instances are to be found not only in the book of Deuteronomy but throughout the Old Testament. These three psalms are powerful chronological hymns.

In all of this Israel learned, and was taught by God, that He required obedience to his repeated saving acts of mercy and deliverance. Israel sinned repeatedly and God showed patience and often anger, but never rejected them at all from his constant care.

Book IV of the Psalter ends at Psalm 106.47 and v. 48 is a doxology or praise item bringing the book to its close. Psalm 106 is the 4th longest psalm.

Psalm 107. For his steadfast love endures for ever!

Book	V
Number of verses	43
Key verse	1*

Type of psalm	Praise, with thanksgiving for deliverance
Possible original usage and setting	Used in Temple worship for thanking God for his goodness and provision
Including prayer or not	Not as a prayer as such but still offered to God
Individual or Communal	Communal
Date and author	An early psalm adopted for later more formal use is a suggestion
Subsequent and Contemporary significance - Messianic indications	The unique narrative presents an appealing picture to its readers. God is good! However, for Christian readers less instructive than many other psalms.

*Key verse is the repeated refrain in verses 1, 8, 15, 21, and 31.

The psalm records the pain of four separate afflicted groups, and records both their deliverance and their subsequent thankfulness to God their deliverer. This psalm marks a grand beginning to Book V, the final collection of psalms in the Psalter. Psalm 107 is not a Davidic psalm but is followed by another two sequences of psalms all bearing David's name in the superscription, Psalms 108-110 and 138–145.

There will also be the Psalms of Ascent 120–134, as well as the Egyptian Hallel 113–118 and the Great Hallel 146–150.

In spite of its limited Christian significance, this psalm could well be acted out as a pageant of God's good works by a progressive and innovative youth group, or even a church session!

Psalm 108

This Psalm is a doublet of Psalms 57.7-11 and 60.5-12 and its message, meaning and measurements are covered under those psalms.

Psalm 109. All about revenge!

Book	V
Number of verses	31
Key verse	6

Type of psalm	Lament
Possible original usage and setting	To elicit God's help against wicked men, unlikely in public worship
Including prayer or not	An intense prayer. Is it legitimate?
Individual or Communal	Individual
Date and author	Post-exilic, anonymous
Subsequent and Contemporary significance - Messianic indications	This psalm and others like it raise questions.

This drama has been acted and re-enacted in every generation, and probably by every believer at some time or other. C. S. Lewis (1958) calls this psalm and others like it, 'the cursings'. The dilemma for God-believing people is that it seems wrong and evil to curse ones' opponents. We do not think it is right, and yet give way to such thoughts if not to corresponding actions.

The psalmists took sin very seriously and believed in God's integrity. If Psalm 88 is the saddest psalm then Psalm 109 is the angriest. The psalmist pleads that God, having dispensed justice and punishment on the miscreant, will now bless and reward and restore and celebrate the suffering psalmist. This is reminiscent of the man Job with all his sufferings in the end being restored and rewarded. (See Job42).

The problem of unmerited suffering is always present, but so too is the presence of evil in the world.

Psalm 110. The Messiah and Melchizedek the priest.

Book	V
Number of verses	7
Key verse	1

Type of psalm	Royal, the ninth of eleven Royal Psalms
Possible original usage and setting	Worship, probably on the anniversary of the king's enthronement, or does it celebrate God's rule?
Including prayer or not	More like prophecy than prayer
Individual or Communal	Individual
Date and author	Pre-exilic and asking the question as to whether this is a psalm about David
Subsequent and Contemporary significance - Messianic indications	This psalm is influential in the New Testament and is quoted often as a messianic psalm.

The interpretation of Psalm 110 has always been contentious and complicated! It is difficult to know who is speaking and to whom. The psalm may be a reference to both King David and the Davidic line of kings. The relationship between Psalm 2 and this psalm is clearly seen. Both psalms encourage the reader, singer and worshipper to ponder the relationship between the divine and the merely human, between the King of kings and the mere king. God's rule, past, present and future is the subject of the psalm and these purposes are worked out through the agency of a King David, although perhaps a later day David.

There are many references in the New Testament to this psalm, not only the Gospels but also in the writings of Paul, the Book of the Acts and the Letter to the Hebrews.

The psalm was hugely important to First Century Christians and has been a key note psalm ever since.

Psalm 111. God's works endure for ever.

Book	V
Number of verses	7
Key verse	6

Type of psalm	Praise
Possible original usage and setting	An acrostic psalm in twenty-two lines, perhaps written for instruction purposes. Other acrostic psalms are 9/10, 34, 37, 111, 119 and 145
Including prayer or not	Not a prayer, more a lesson
Individual or Communal	The individual perhaps speaks for the class
Date and author	Post exilic, author unknown
Subsequent and Contemporary significance - Messianic indications	A very appropriate psalm for the Christian era

This is a Praise psalm which also bears the marks of the Wisdom movement and has similarities to the Book of Proverbs, which is the classic Wisdom text in the Bible. verse. 10 is the keynote Wisdom motif, "the fear of the Lord is the beginning of wisdom". The two key words in this psalm are 'works' and 'covenant', the former appearing five times. This is reminiscent of the Christian prayer:

By the prayers of Jesus, Lord teach us to pray; by the works of Jesus, Lord teach us to work; by the gifts of Jesus Lord teach us to give; by the love of Jesus, Lord teach us to love, and by the Cross of Jesus, Lord teach us to live. Amen.

(Author unknown used by D Arnott 2017 personal communication).

This emphasis on works in this psalm accords well with both the Jewish and Christian work ethics.

Psalm 112. The reward of the godly man.

Book	V
Number of verses	19
Key verse	1

Type of psalm	Wisdom, seventh of eleven. The others are 1, 32, 37, 49, 73,78, 119, 127, 128 and 133
Possible original usage and setting	Possibly for teaching. Another acrostic psalm
Including prayer or not	Not a prayer but a lesson
Individual or Communal	Individual, or perhaps teacher to pupil
Date and author	Probably late post-exilic
Subsequent and Contemporary significance - Messianic indications	Clearly Saint Paul was an ardent student of the psalms See 2 Corinthians 9.9

Psalm 111 and 112 have similarities, although one is Praise and the other Wisdom, they both commend the wise way to live and advertise its benefits, and both are acrostic. Psalms 37,112, 119 are both acrostic and Wisdom.

If Proverbs 31 is the portrait of the perfect wife and mother then indeed Psalm 112 is the portrait of the 'ideal' or model man. Here is the devout man who was also worldly wise. Here is the good Israelite/ Jew who is also a world citizen. His rewards will be great in this world and the next! In the final verse the psalmist/ wise man who wrote the psalm cannot resist this condemnation of the 'wicked' in the land.

If there is any possible criticism of such a wise man it must surely be that he is as much self-satisfied as God- satisfied! He seems to attribute a great deal of his success to himself.

Psalm 113. Praise the name of the Lord.

Book	V
Number of verses	9
Key verse	4

Type of psalm	Praise. First of the Egyptian Hallel psalms
Possible original usage and setting	In worship at the great festivals e.g. Passover, in the praise of God, and continuing at the synagogue
Including prayer or not	Not a prayer but a hymn
Individual or Communal	Communal
Date and author	Probably post-exilic
Subsequent and Contemporary significance - Messianic indications	It is in the Psalms that Jews and Christian probably come closest together.

Psalm 113 is the first of the Egyptian Hallel series (113–118). They were all sung at the feast of the Passover, which is celebrated in the homes of the people (whereas the other great festivals were all Temple centred and are now synagogue centred). All the Hallel psalms are about God delivering his promises to his people. These psalms can be very charismatic in their performance when sung with total commitment and the participation by the congregation. Again, this is a point of meeting for Jew and Christian: both celebrate these psalms with total participation. This psalm is an invitation to uninhibited worship of voices, minds and our whole beings. With the work begun by Iain Whyte, the well-known 20th century hymn writer, there does seem to be a resurgence of psalms being sung with joy and enthusiasm (Church Hymnary CH4 2007).

Psalms 113-118 comprise a collection called the Egyptian Hallel (Kidner D 1973 & A. A. Anderson 1972).

Psalm 114. Israel after the Exodus.

Book	V
Number of verses	8
Key verse	8

Type of psalm	Praise
Possible original usage and setting	Thanksgiving worship in song accompanied by musical instruments (see Psalm 150)
Including prayer or not	Not a prayer, more a rustic idyll
Individual or Communal	Communal
Date and author	Probably pre-exilic. No author designated in the superscription
Subsequent and Contemporary significance - Messianic indications	A quiet psalm of reflective thanksgiving. Traditionally sung by Jews on the eighth day of the Passover.

This little psalm suggests a variety of subjects. It may be about the Exodus from Egypt, or the crossing of the sea, or the crossing of the Jordan, or God forming the mountains at creation, or God providing precious water to thirsty people? Or is Psalm 114 simply an invitation to meditate on the power of God?

It is certainly about deliverance from slavery to freedom. Indeed, it is akin to the Christian negro spiritual "Tell me the old, old story". The psalm powerfully says, *"Look and see what God has done"*.

The psalm is not typical Temple language as it is much more a folk song in the guise of a psalm. Israel's history reduced to eight short verses.

Psalm 115. Our God and their gods.

Book	V
Number of verses	18
Key verses	3&4

Type of psalm	Praise
Possible original usage and setting	Used in worship liturgy to help overcome a fear of foreign gods
Including prayer or not	Prayer possibly used responsively, priest leading and congregation responding
Individual or Communal	Communal in the congregation
Date and author	Post-exilic is indicated from the language used. Author unknown
Subsequent and Contemporary significance - Messianic indications	The enthusiasm of Psalm 115 will be infectious in any era

The spontaneous gratitude is a joy to read. For Jewish, and subsequently for Christian congregations this will have been good to read and to hear and to share. This psalm pours their heartfelt thanks to an all-providing God.

The psalm is a thoroughgoing denunciation of foreign, and by implication false, gods and their idols. This denunciation is reminiscent of the prophets Isaiah, Amos Hosea and Micah.

"Israel" or "Aaron" and the specific definitions of what constitutes these groups is obscure or at least ambiguous because we are given no clue as to the author's identity or authority. What is very clear is that this psalm encompasses all who would draw near to God, whether Israelite or adherent.

Many psalms address both the people Israel and all who fear the Lord.

The confidence exuding from this glorious hymn has been recognised for many centuries.

Psalm 116. What shall I render to the Lord?

Book	V
Number of verses	19
Key verse	13

Type of psalm	Praise
Possible original usage and setting	A public recital of gratitude, Temple use and other
Including prayer or not	Public acknowledgement of gratitude with v. 8 and 16 explicit prayer
Individual or Communal	An individual expresses his gratitude in the company of a congregation
Date and author	The use of Aramaic in the original Hebrew indicates a late post-exilic date
Subsequent and Contemporary significance - Messianic indications	In the Reformed Church the passage became an integral part of the Holy Communion service

It is good for all people to count their blessings from time to time, and this psalm does just that. The psalm is a really powerful statement of both faith and gratitude to God. This psalm is unique in several ways. The words "I" and "my" are used about 20 times, making the psalm both intensely personal and also strongly declaratory. This is a psalmist who, through good times and bad, recognises his indebtedness to God and declares the same to all who hear him. It is a marvellous faith declaration.

It is a remarkable 'drawing near to God' psalm. The psalm amounts to a full confession of faith before the whole congregation.

Psalm 116.10 is quoted in 2 Corinthians 4.13.

Psalm 117. Praise the Lord all nations.

Book	V
Number of verses	2
Key verse	2

Type of psalm	Praise
Possible original usage and setting	Possibly used in Temple liturgy
Including prayer or not	Not a prayer but a shout of praise
Individual or Communal	Communal
Date and author	Post-exilic date with author unknown
Subsequent and Contemporary significance - Messianic indications	Is it liturgy or personal acclamation?

Psalm 117 is the shortest psalm. Psalm 119 is the longest at 176 verses. This is a hymn not only for Israel but also for all the nations. Although the Jews were not much concerned about other nations and their gods, they nevertheless from time to time proclaimed their Yahweh (LORD) as the God of all nations and all people; this is the message of this delightful little hymn of praise. Derek Kidner (1973) in the Tyndale Commentary series says, "This tiny psalm is great in faith." "All peoples" and "endures for ever" are two wonderfully comprehensive phrases (pg. 411). A. A. Anderson (1972) in the New Century Bible Commentary series comments "when Saint Paul cites Psalm 117 in Romans 15.11 he did so to 'prove' that the inclusion of the gentiles was in the divine programme" (pg. 796). The comprehensiveness of the little psalm with only 39 words (in English) is striking!

Psalm 118. This is the day that the Lord has made.

Book	V
Number of verses	29
Key verse	22

Type of psalm	Praise, final psalm of the Egyptian Hallel (Psalms 113–118)
Possible original usage and setting	Thought to have been used at the Feast of Tabernacles in the Temple or at its gates
Including prayer or not	Prayer and thanksgiving
Individual or Communal	Although a congregational hymn it is also personal, so both individual and communal
Date and author	Post-exilic
Subsequent and Contemporary significance - Messianic indications	Jew and Christian will hear this psalm messianically, of the One to come

Psalm 118 is a very significant for Christians on account of v.22-23 being quoted in Matthew, Mark and Luke as well as the Acts of the Apostles, and v.25-26 being quoted in all four Gospels. It is one of the most quoted psalms in the New Testament. Psalms 110 and 118 feature very often in congregational public prayers.

The psalm is a liturgy of thanksgiving and verse 19 seems most comprehensively to declare that gratitude. There are many memorable verses but it is perhaps the phrase *"his steadfast love endures for ever"* that comes to mind most readily. Indeed, the phrase, although not occurring in all of the Egyptian Hallel psalms, does express their message.

The psalm is also similar in language to Psalm 136 which features the same refrain.

Psalm 119. A eulogy on the Law of the Lord.

Book	V
Number of verses	176
Key verse	33

Type of psalm	Wisdom, the eighth of eleven wisdom psalms, viz. Psalms 1, 32, 37, 49, 73,78, 112, 119, 127, 128, and 133
Possible original usage and setting	Probably used by the Wisdom teachers in their instruction the young and non-Jewish adherents
Including prayer or not	The whole psalm is set down as a prayer
Individual or Communal	Individual and applicable to all individuals
Date and author	Post-exilic
Subsequent and Contemporary significance - Messianic indications	Can be compared to discipleship hymns such as 'Fight the good fight' and 'Onward Christian soldiers'

The longest psalm is a 22 part acrostic poem with the first word of each part beginning with successive letters of the Hebrew alphabet. Other acrostic psalms have the letters beginning successive verses in Psalms 25, 34, 37,111,112 and 145. As has been mentioned earlier, the acrostic effect is not discerned in English.

The 22 parts have much in common with the focus being upon the Law of God. That Law is described by nine synonyms for law: word, statute, testimony, precepts, commandments, judgments, ways and ordinances. These are all used almost interchangeably. The total effect is to commend the law, encourage adherence to it, to relate it to the reader or student as God's law and thus beyond either criticism, change, or addition. The law is the sum of all divine revelation and is the precious gift of God

The role of Psalm 119 in the Old Testament is comparable to that of the Beatitudes in the New Testament: two very different documents yet both declaring God's precious life-giving gifts.

Psalm 120. Confessions of a peace worker!

Book	V
Number of verses	7
Key verse	7

Type of psalm	Lament
Possible original usage and setting	Pilgrims, perhaps from Babylon, going up to the great religious festivals in the Jerusalem Temple
Including prayer or not	Not a prayer
Individual or Communal	Individual, yet sung by many pilgrims
Date and author	Post-exilic
Subsequent and Contemporary significance - Messianic indications	The fifteen Psalms of Ascent (120 - 134) formed a well-defined group and have always been much used in Christian praise. The mention of peace may be a messianic longing.

These Songs of Ascent form the best defined psalm collection in the Psalter. Their varied subjects and types may indicate that they were compiled into this group at a much later date than their date of writing.

Specifically, there is no pilgrimage vocabulary in Psalm 120 which seems more like an anthem for peace workers. Not only will those who live in Ireland or the Republic of South Africa or Palestine or Syria, but all who sympathise with them, will identify with v. 6-7.

There seems to be no mention of 'going up' in this psalm and it does not fit easily with some of the other Songs of Ascent.

Psalm 121. I lift up my eyes to the hills.

Book	V
Number of verses	8
Key verse	8

Type of psalm	Praise, one of fifteen Songs of Ascent
Possible original usage and setting	An entrance liturgy to the Temple or a pilgrims' travelling hymn on the way to Jerusalem
Including prayer or not	Not a prayer
Individual or Communal	Individual and reply
Date and author	Post-exilic, author unknown
Subsequent and Contemporary significance - Messianic indications	Psalm 121 is a most popular Christian hymn.

The second Song of Ascent is easily identified as a Pilgrim Song and immediately teaches the traveller that his help comes from God and not the hills, which may be a reference to the worship of 'high' places by some of Israel's historic contemporaries. This psalm has been at times carelessly understood to suggest that the hills help the fugitive. Psalm 11.1 corrects the risk of any such confusion.

The psalm is a dialogue probably between a worshipper and a priest or perhaps between a father and his son or between groups of travellers as they walked. Whatever the original understanding, Christians have sung the psalm albeit with a different set of pre-suppositions but nevertheless with a similar need for solace and guidance on the way.

Psalm 122. Prayer for the peace of Jerusalem.

Book	V
Number of verses	9
Key verse	6

Type of psalm	Praise
Possible original usage and setting	Sung both at the annual festivals but also as pilgrims made their way to Jerusalem for them
Including prayer or not	Both a song and a prayer
Individual or Communal	Begins with an individual and then embraces others.
Date and author	Post-exilic
Subsequent and Contemporary significance - Messianic indications	For pilgrims and returnees such a psalm has much meaning for both Jews and Christians

If Psalm 120 was the trials of the expatriate and Psalm 121 the hazards of the traveller then Psalm 122 is the joy of arrival! (Kidner D 1973). In the many centuries since this song was first sung, it has been prayed many millions of times, not only for the peace of Jerusalem but for the peace of many other Jerusalems. Indeed, many pious people, not only Jews and Christians, will have used these words to ask for God's blessing on their own particular place. The final two verses of the letter of Jude in the New Testament fulfil something similar in more specific Christian language.

The original psalm was one of national thanksgiving but from individuals to nations the same words are applicable and powerful and have so very often been wonderfully uplifting and reassuring. The words translate easily across all centuries, climates and boundaries.

Psalm 123. Eyes to the Lord!

Book	V
Number of verses	4
Key verse	2

Type of psalm	Lament
Possible original usage and setting	More a psalm for the home than the sanctuary
Including prayer or not	Prayer
Individual or Communal	Individual and family perhaps
Date and author	Post-exilic perhaps the time of Nehemiah (fifth or fourth century BC)
Subsequent and Contemporary significance - Messianic indications	A psalm of domestic significance in every age

This is the fourth Song of Ascent, and it almost seems to have been written for those who were left at home and did not get to go to the Festival in Jerusalem. God is the hope of the weak and this is a plea for grace, especially for the servants who do not get a big exposure in the Psalter. And remarkably perhaps it is a plea for the female servants, however unlikely this might be for the fourth century BC. Who then are the proud and arrogant? The answer will depend on whose eyes are doing the watching. It may well be that without straining the rules of Bible study too much this is a very modern psalm!

This then may be what gives Psalm 123 its unique importance in the Psalter and its contemporary significance.

Psalm 124. Our help is in the name of the Lord.

Book	V
Number of verses	8
Key verse	8

Type of psalm	Praise
Possible original usage and setting	Sung antiphonally in liturgical worship
Including prayer or not	Prayer and praise
Individual or Communal	Communal ("our")
Date and author	Post-exilic, by a now unknown author
Subsequent and Contemporary significance - Messianic indications	Psalm 124 gave rise to a very popular metrical psalm, "Now Israel may say and that truly"

This psalm raises many questions. Who were the attackers? What was the flood mentioned in v. 4? From whom did the victims escape? There are so many questions and so few answers. Any number of assailants or natural disasters could have befallen these pilgrims as they travelled. There is great joy (praise) as they arrive safely. Different authorities have offered different original historical situations out of which thus psalm might have arisen. The psalm as it is now recorded is the fifth of the Songs of Ascent and it is such a wonderful expression of both the joy and the gratitude with which pilgrims would have arrived for the festivals in Jerusalem.

A modern paraphrase of the psalm is expressed in the John Bell hymn, "Now let God's people. Let God's Israel witness the truth and gratefully proclaim." (Church Hymnary CH4 2007 Hymn 85)

Thanks, is not specifically articulated but the psalm exudes gratitude, it breathes a spirit of thankfulness to God.

Psalm 125. God's protection is around his faithful.

Book	V
Number of verses	5
Key verse	1

Type of psalm	Praise, with overtones of Wisdom
Possible original usage and setting	In the liturgy of the Temple and by the pilgrims as they made their way to Jerusalem possibly for the New Year Festival
Including prayer or not	Narrative and prayer
Individual or Communal	Communal.
Date and author	Post–exilic, the language reinforces this view
Subsequent and Contemporary significance - Messianic indications	This may well have been the message of the Temple priests at the festival

This is the sixth Song of Ascent although the final phrase seems like a later addition comparable to the greeting "Peace be with you". This is a psalm about providence, about God providing for his people, Israel, either in the provision of a victory for by rescuing them from trouble. It reads like a national psalm of trust within the 'type' of Praise. The phrase "the sceptre of wickedness" may refer to foreign or pagan influence in Israel. However, the pervasiveness of sin and evil is not the sole fault of the foreigners or entirely due to their influence. Sin is part of the universal human condition.

This psalm reinforces Jewish orthodoxy; the good are rewarded and sin deserves punishment.

This phrase is quoted in a slightly fuller form in Galatians 6.16.

Psalm 126. Restore our fortunes O Lord.

Book	V
Number of verses	6
Key verse	3

Type of psalm	Lament
Possible original usage and setting	Autumn Festival in the Jerusalem Temple or the Feast of Tabernacles
Including prayer or not	Prayer
Individual or Communal	Communal
Date and author	Post-exilic. Psalmist unknown
Subsequent and Contemporary significance - Messianic indications	Christians use the psalm and many will regard it as messianic

This short Song of Ascent cumulatively reinforces the unique relationship of Yahweh (the LORD) to Israel. Some scholars argue for a re-arrangement of the verses with v. 1-3 following v. 4-6. However, the argument for such a change is no more compelling than leaving well alone!

In this psalm the writer may be reflecting upon the joy of the returning exiles from Babylon to Jerusalem in the sixth century BC, or may be a prophetic priest's prayer for restoration.

If so, is it a prayer for restoration in the future, or for long past deliverance? On balance, it would seem more likely that this is a prayer of thanksgiving for mercies granted in the past.

A modern rendering of the psalm as Hymn 86 in the Church of Scotland's Church Hymnary CH4 2007 makes the assumption that deliverance has been effected, and the psalm is turned into a Harvest Thanksgiving hymn.

Psalm 127. Unless the Lord builds the house.

Book	V
Number of verses	5
Key verse	1

Type of psalm	Wisdom, ninth of eleven Wisdom psalms
Possible original usage and setting	Perhaps at the Feast of Tabernacles and certainly for teaching
Including prayer or not	Probably a responsive prayer
Individual or Communal	Communal
Date and author	Post-exilic most likely. Solomon unlikely to be author
Subsequent and Contemporary significance - Messianic indications	Messianic interpretation possible and this psalm has been used in Christian liturgy on Iona

Psalm 127 is a powerful testimony to the well-led life. It is also a difficult hymn for single women and those couples unable to have children. Whereas v. 1-2 are received joyously by everyone, v. 3-5 are more difficult to sing, read or pray.

The reference to building may well account for the reference to Solomon in the superscription.

In v. 1, house is a metaphor for building, or an individual life or for the life of a family. It is on this basis that the two halves of the psalm are held together. Otherwise it is difficult to relate the first two verses to the latter three.

The psalm is appropriate for responsive prayer. When the Iona Abbey was being restored in the second half of the twentieth century it was very moving to listen to the Community members intone v. 1 every morning before continuing work on the re-building.

199

Psalm 128. The blessings of a God–fearing man.

Book	V
Number of verses	6
Key verse	1

Type of psalm	Wisdom - tenth of eleven.
Possible original usage and setting	Perhaps a priestly blessing at the Feast of Tabernacles
Including prayer or not	Not a prayer addressed directly to God
Individual or Communal	Communal
Date and author	Probably post-exilic, author an anonymous Wise man
Subsequent and Contemporary significance - Messianic indications	Psalm 128 has been proved true throughout the centuries for many people

This is the ninth Song of Ascent, and a prayer and song for the welfare of Jerusalem and all Israel. Martin Luther called it "a marriage song" and the pair of psalms, 127 and 128, are similar in content.

The first verse could well be seen as a forerunner of the first beatitude, (Matthew 5.3) especially in the New English Bible Translation. Derek Kidner (1973) calls the mood of this psalm one of contented piety.

The word 'fears' occurs in both v.1 and 4 and the modern understanding of that word is more negative than the intended meaning of 'respect'. To respect, honour, obey, serve, are all closer in meaning than the more negative 'fear' of the Lord.

Both Psalms 127 and 128 are very family orientated. The psalmist passes easily from the family to the nation as a larger family.

Psalm 129. Beware, Zion's enemies!

Book	V
Number of verses	8
Key verse	1

Type of psalm	Praise, but in a negative vein.
Possible original usage and setting	While v.1-4 are thanksgiving, v. 5-8 are for revenge
Including prayer or not	Not a prayer
Individual or Communal	Communal for Israel
Date and author	Post-exilic, author unknown
Subsequent and Contemporary significance - Messianic indications	This is a very sad tenth Song of Ascent, almost a song of the persecuted.

The Israelites would need to have been careful where they sang this particular song. Certainly, it is not a song for a mixed community of Jews and Gentiles! It is also a sad psalm and does not seem to fit easily into the joy and celebratory mood of the pilgrims coming up to Jerusalem (but then several of these Songs of Ascent were not the fervent rejoicing of happy pilgrims). This makes the reader remember that these collections were made a long time ago and we are no longer aware of the selection criteria.

Verses 1 and 2 illustrate well the leader/ priest intoning the first phrase, and the congregation responding and they also illustrate well the parallelism of Hebrew poetry.

Psalm 130. Are you listening, Lord?

Book	V
Number of verses	8
Key verse	3

Type of psalm	Lament
Possible original usage and setting	In worship at the annual festivals in the Jerusalem Temple
Including prayer or not	Prayer
Individual or Communal	For the individual and the community (v. 7& 8)
Date and author	Post-exilic, author unknown
Subsequent and Contemporary significance - Messianic indications	Christians know this psalm as one of the seven Penitential Psalms (others are 6, 32, 38, 51, 102 and 143). To this day it is widely sung in churches.

Psalms 143 and 130 form a pair as they have much in common (see Psalm 143).

This psalm, which is quoted in both Romans and Galatians and is one of those Martin Luther referred to as his Pauline Psalms, is also the final Song of Ascent (Ps 121-130) (Anderson AA 1972). The pair are thought to have been sung by the faithful as they journeyed to Jerusalem for the great annual festivals or as the worshipers went up the actual temple steps. Although these psalms often speak of distressing situations, the very acts of saying and singing and praying them will often lead the worshipper from despair to hope. W. H. Bellinger (2012) writes, "these psalms are honest pilgrimage songs and they deal with all of life" (pg. 148).

Thank you Lord, for listening to all my prayers. Thank you for forgiving my sins. Thank you for being the hope of the world and my hope. Grant to us the patience required to wait upon the Lord and renew our strength. In Jesus' Name, Amen.

(Gordon R 2003)

Psalm 131. Child-like trust in God.

Book	V
Number of verses	3
Key verse	2

Type of psalm	Praise
Possible original usage and setting	For personal use and spiritual development
Including prayer or not	Prayer
Individual or Communal	Individual
Date and author	Post-exilic, author unknown
Subsequent and Contemporary significance - Messianic indications	Verse. 3 seems to introduce a messianic dimension

This is a short and deceptively simple poem, which in reality is a very profound psalm and is somehow reminiscent of the parable of the two men who went up to the Temple to pray (see Luke 18.10 ff). One was proud and loud, the other humble and contrite. Lord help us to be such! Psalm 131 is about personal faith, about growing in grace, about humility and devotion.

This is a spiritual exercise and when that exercise is over the psalmist then prays for his nation and his people and extends the prayer to encompass a future as well as a present reference.

It may be that not only does this devout soul pray this at home, but also as he travels and as he arrives in Jerusalem.

Does Psalm 131 anticipate Matthew 18.1-4, where Jesus teaches the nature of real greatness?

Psalm 131 is one of the four shortest psalms. Psalm 117 is the shortest, and Psalms 131, 133 and 134 are all about the same length.

Psalm 132. God's covenant with David's dynasty.

Book	V
Number of verses	18
Key verse	12

Type of psalm	Royal Psalm, tenth of eleven, others are 2, 18, 20, 21, 45, 72, 89, 101, 110, and 144
Possible original usage and setting	Originally used when the Ark of the Covenant was brought to Jerusalem for a Festival of Dedication perhaps the Autumn Festival.
Including prayer or not	Prayer and narrative
Individual or Communal	Individual in the name of the king
Date and author	Pre-exilic, traditionally David wrote this psalm
Subsequent and Contemporary significance - Messianic indications	Used infrequently

Although this psalm is about both the human king (David and his successors) it is also about God as Israel's ultimate sovereign. These eleven Royal Psalms are about the actual human kings of Israel and Judah. This psalm idealises David and there is a glossing over of his falls from grace. It was David who established the pattern of a Davidic line and there are many references throughout the Old Testament to God choosing David and his line to reign forever. Psalm 132 appears to be a primary source and one with a long history. Perhaps not written in David's own time but written much earlier than the Songs of Ascent (Ps 120-134).

David is remembered fondly from that generation to this one as the Father of Judaism. His people to this day are the people of David, and of course Jesus' own human ancestry was traced back through the Davidic line (see Acts 2.30).

Psalm 133. Families are precious!

Book	V
Number of verses	3
Key verse	1

Type of psalm	Wisdom, the first Wisdom Psalm
Possible original usage and setting	Various suggestions are current, including that the psalm may have been a greeting when visiting
Including prayer or not	Not a prayer
Individual or Communal	Communal, presumably in a family setting
Date and author	Post-exilic, author unknown
Subsequent and Contemporary significance - Messianic indications	A universal truth for all healthy communities, either Jewish or Christian. The final words suggest a messianic aspect for the psalm

This short psalm celebrates the fellowship of the covenant people in Jerusalem and rejoices and revels with the faith community. All the Israelite males were brothers in God's sight and this psalm acknowledges that. The beauty of living together in harmony is both a prayer for today and also a Messianic expectation.

The implications of such a statement for all faith communities and for all faith families ever since are clear. This is how God wants it to be!

There is a similarity between this psalm and Psalm 1. Both of them urge God's people to be a family in the very best understanding of that title. The imagery of the beard and the collar may be lost on our generation but there is no doubt about the meaning.

The psalm is written in celebratory mode and the Wise sage who wrote the psalm has left a beautiful blueprint of how things should be.

Psalm 134. A night hymn.

Book	V
Number of verses	3
Key verse	1

Type of psalm	Praise
Possible original usage and setting	In the Temple, at the Feast of Tabernacles, by night
Including prayer or not	Not a prayer but a hymn
Individual or Communal	Communal, priests and congregation
Date and author	Post-exilic, author unknown
Subsequent and Contemporary significance - Messianic indications	Justifying evening services – late night worship can be very special

This is the final Song of Ascent, the fifteenth of fifteen. They included Praise, Lament and two Wisdom psalms. It may be that the first two verses are an exhortation to the priests to be faithful and the final verse serves as a doxology for the Songs of Ascent collection or as the priestly blessing of the people who were at worship. The Levitical singers did duty twenty-four hours a day, in shifts, so that the sound of praise was never quiet in the Temple. The details are in the Book of Chronicles (1 Chronicles 25).

Worship and obedience are the proper response to God's grace by all people at all times. This little hymn reminds all who read it or hear it or sing it.

For the pilgrims who had come up to Jerusalem for the Feast, this psalm perhaps represents their final visit to the Temple before a few hours' sleep, and departure early the following morning for the long journey home.

Psalm 135. A plethora of praise.

Book	V
Number of verses	21
Key verse	5

Type of psalm	Praise
Possible original usage and setting	The Feast of the Passover has been suggested
Including prayer or not	Praise and prayer
Individual or Communal	Communal
Date and author	Late post-exilic
Subsequent and Contemporary significance - Messianic indications	Psalm 113 and 135 are both about a saviour God. This is a psalm with a messianic emphasis.

The Psalms 121-136 form a group which can be entitled the Pilgrim Songs. Psalm 135 is possibly the most comprehensive hymn of praise in the whole Old Testament. There is creation history here and salvation history and, as indicated above, the future reference is also present. There are echoes of the prophets, especially in v. 15-18, and the entire psalm reverberates with the joy of communal praise.

Psalm 135 appears to be one of the most comprehensive of all the psalms in the range of subject matter that is covered. Derek Kidner (1973) uses the phrase, "an anthology of praise", almost an encyclopaedia of praise! (pg. 455).

The psalm may be a mosaic gathered from other psalms such as Psalms 115 and 136, and yet the result is a coherent item of praise.

Idols are knocked or mocked and yet as we know every generation has its own idols; the Second Commandment is therefore as necessary today as it ever was ("Thou shalt not make for yourself a graven image" (or idol) Exodus Ch. 20 v 4f.)

Psalm 136. For His steadfast love endures for ever.

Book	V
Number of verses	26
Key verse	26

Type of psalm	Praise
Possible original usage and setting	The Temple and synagogue and possibly for the Feast of the Passover.
Including prayer or not	This is a hymn for singing in two parts, not a prayer
Individual or Communal	Communal
Date and author	Late post-exilic reflecting a more developed liturgical practice
Subsequent and Contemporary significance - Messianic indications	This classic responsive hymn is still in common use in Christian churches

This is a somewhat repetitive psalm to say or sing in parts, with the priest or leader taking the odd-numbered lines and the congregation responding every time with "for his steadfast love endures for ever". Nevertheless, history is revised, and the worshippers are powerfully reminded of God as the Lord of both creation and history. And at the end of the psalm there is also the universal dimension of God's love and care when God provides food for all flesh (v. 25).

In the Psalter, there are different Hallel Psalms e.g. the Egyptian Hallel Psalms 113– 118 and the Great Hallel Psalms 120–136. The term means Hallelujah or simply, "Praise the Lord!".

The dominant notes are thanksgiving, acknowledgement, and confession of all that God is and all that God has done.

Psalm 137. By the waters of Babylon.

Book	V
Number of verses	9
Key verse	4

Type of psalm	Lament - an imprecation
Possible original usage and setting	To give vent to natural emotion and leave it with God
Including prayer or not	More like a curse than a prayer leaving it with God
Individual or Communal	One person is speaking and giving vent to the anger and pain of the nation
Date and author	Written in Babylon and difficult to know who it is and who is speaking to whom
Subsequent and Contemporary significance - Messianic indications	This is the classic responsive psalm. This remains a contemporary issue to praise God in a foreign environment!

The psalm remains a contemporary issue as it is never easy to worship in a foreign environment particularly one that is antagonistic or one that repudiates the worshippers' beliefs.

This is as bitter as any of the 'cursing psalms' and Christians find such naked aggression difficult to handle. Yet this is how they felt and how many Christians have felt but not expressed it in the face of cruelty, torture or persecution. The solution is left in the hands of God and it is God who is beseeched to restore all things. The majority of the laments are individual but this Lament Psalm is a communal lament.

Is there a positive message in all of this? Yes, for the believer, "God is always near me."

Psalm 138. Confidence in God.

Book	V
Number of verses	8
Key verse	4

Type of psalm	Praise
Possible original usage and setting	Thanksgiving of the community, expressed through the psalmist's words
Including prayer or not	Prayer
Individual or Communal	Individual
Date and author	Post-exilic like most of Book V but author unknown. Probably fifth century BC
Subsequent and Contemporary significance - Messianic indications	Giving rise to Christian praise and messianic implications

The psalm expresses thanks to God after deliverance from the Babylonian Exile. This is the first psalm since Psalm 110 attributed to David in the superscription and now the next nine will be attributed to him. As has been mentioned elsewhere the term 'of David' is open to variable understandings and now, so many centuries after both the writing and the collecting and the compiling of the five books comprising the Psalter, dogmatic assertions are difficult to confirm.

The psalm is complicated by the fact that v. 1-3 and 7- 8 are in the singular whereas v. 4-6 are in the plural. This raises the possibility of the present psalm having arisen from two separate sources.

Psalm 138 remains a beautiful and moving song of thanks being expressed to God, and as such is applicable in any century in any context. Many Christians will want to understand the psalm referring forward in time to the Messiah.

Psalm 139. Portrait of a man close to God.

Book	V
Number of verses	24
Key verse	1

Type of psalm	Praise
Possible original usage and setting	Non liturgical use, i.e. not in the Temple
Including prayer or not	Prayer
Individual or Communal	Individual
Date and author	Post-exilic, author unknown
Subsequent and Contemporary significance - Messianic indications	Hugely important in Christian worship e.g. in Church of Scotland's Church Hymnary CH4 (2007) Hymns 96 and 97 are much used

The psalm comes in two parts, v. 1-18 are heartfelt thanksgiving and v.19–24 are a hate prayer on the evildoers. Thus, the psalm is both praise and a curse. The unity of the psalm is questioned by some, but A. A. Anderson (1972) and others accept it as the work of one psalmist.

Whereas the first part is majestic praise, the second part demonstrates almost perfect hatred and so Psalm 139 is a classic 'cursing psalm'. C.S. Lewis (1958) has helped many to receive and accept these psalms, but it nevertheless expresses a kind of raw hatred that is difficult to receive. The psalmist expects God to be the agent of destruction.

As is often the case the final two verses somewhat redeem the situation and the psalm ends on a positive note.

The variety of the interpretations suggested by the scholars is wide and leaves the reader free to wonder and to ponder.

Psalm 140. Deliver me O God from evil men.

Book	V
Number of verses	13
Key verse	7

Type of psalm	Lament
Possible original usage and setting	The prayer of an accused man, a request for God's righteous judgement
Including prayer or not	Prayer
Individual or Communal	Individual
Date and author	Fourth or third century BC and under the superscription of David
Subsequent and Contemporary significance - Messianic indications	This psalm will never have been easy to read, and will always be topical.

There are echoes of other psalms and other portions of the Old Testament to be found in Psalm 140 substantiating the suggestion of a late date. The Psalm is also quoted in Romans 3.10-18.

The psalmist is very conscious of evil, and of violent and wicked men, all of whom seek his downfall or worse. He does not hold back on the evil he would desire for them! "May they roast in hell" would be a fair paraphrase.

Is the psalmist in the dock as an accused man? If so he is making an appeal to the Righteous Judge and v. 11-12 express confidence that God will establish justice.

We breathe a sigh of relief! However, the purpose and significance of such a psalm is not easily appreciated. Yet this is how it is! This is the real world with all its pain, and like Saint Paul, while being aware of Psalm 140 and the world it describes, we too are lifted up from such, and the psalmist allows the light to shine again in v. 12-13. This psalm is not easy to read.

Psalm 141. The evening sacrifice.

Book	V
Number of verses	10
Key verse	6

Type of psalm	Lament with evidence of wisdom influence
Possible original usage and setting	At the evening sacrifice in the Temple. (v. 2)
Including prayer or not	Responsive prayer which the priest would have led and to which the congregation would have responded
Individual or Communal	Individual prayer, by each altogether!
Date and author	Post-exilic, unknown author
Subsequent and Contemporary significance - Messianic indications	We are reminded that in the Jerusalem Temple there were sacrifices made every morning and every evening

Although this is a lament the sub plot is that of wisdom – how a good man is required to behave. There are similarities to Psalm 1, which is a full blown Wisdom Psalm. Verse 5 is reminiscent of the Book of Proverbs 9.8, "do not reprove a scoffer or he will hate you". This psalm does call down evil on the wicked but here is the honesty of the psalmist. C.S. Lewis (1958) says of these psalms, which he terms as cursing psalms, "sometimes, in fact often, the psalms hit all their readers where it hurts" (pg. 20f).

Psalm 141.2 is quoted in Revelation 5.8 and 8.3-4.

Psalm 142. Bring me out of prison!

Book	V
Number of verses	7
Key verse	5

Type of psalm	Lament
Possible original usage and setting	Unlikely to have been a Temple psalm, personal devotion seems a more probable original use
Including prayer or not	Prayer
Individual or Communal	Individual
Date and author	A late date seems most likely. Anonymous.
Subsequent and Contemporary significance - Messianic indications	Many unlawfully detained believers will have taken courage from these short verses.

This psalm is very personal and very individualistic. Its 7 painful verses are among the saddest in the Psalter, and must represent a low point in the poet's life. However as is almost always the case the psalm manages to end on an upbeat note. It appears to be more for private meditation rather than public worship.

If the word 'prison' in v. 7 is taken literally then we have a falsely accused innocent victim. If, however it is metaphorical then we have a deeply depressed, disturbed patient calling for God's healing.

The words, sad as they are, and whatever their meaning, are probably everyone's experience at some time. In a sense, all have been there at some time! The psalm may not often be read, however by reading it from time to time, whether or not it applies personally, may encourage the   reader to be more sensitive and caring for a hurting friend.

214

Psalm 143. Teach me, O Lord.

Book	V
Number of verses	12
Key verse	6

Type of psalm	Lament
Possible original usage and setting	An evening prayer in the Temple
Including prayer or not	Prayer
Individual or Communal	Although individual possibly liturgical in use
Date and author	Late post-exilic; author unknown*
Subsequent and Contemporary significance - Messianic indications	One of the seven Penitential Psalms as designated by Christian churches (others are 6, 32, 38, 51, 102, 130)

Not a popular psalm and seldom read in church but certainly used appreciably by solitary souls seeking their way. It may be that the two psalmists who wrote this psalm and Psalm 130 knew of each other and they appear to have quoted from each other.

Psalm 130.3 *'if thou Lord should mark iniquity, who could stand?'*

Psalm 143.2 *'for no man living is righteous before thee'*

Or is it possible that one person wrote both psalms?

In the metrical version of Psalm 143 the line occurs *"Hear my pray O Lord; Give ear to my supplications"* and in every strand of the Old Testament v. 9 is echoed, *"Teach me O Lord the way I should go"*.

This is a quiet psalm, and good that it was recited in the Temple (and presumably) and still in the synagogue. Would that it was read more in Christian churches!

* Although apparently written late yet it is difficult to deny the apparent mark of Davidic authorship.

Psalm 144. God in nature, in history and in providence.

Book	V
Number of verses	15
Key verse	15

Type of psalm	The final Royal psalm of eleven, with overtones of other types, e.g. Lamentation and Praise. See Ps 2,18,20,21, 45,72,89,101,110,132&144.
Possible original usage and setting	The Feast of Tabernacles is possible
Including prayer or not	Includes prayer
Individual or Communal	Individual
Date and author	Date and authorship are debated. Little agreement. It is certainly about David, his poetry and his pilgrimage
Subsequent and Contemporary significance - Messianic indications	Strong messianic implications for Jews and Christians

Here is a psalm about which the scholars suggest a whole gamut of interpretations! The unity of the psalm is debated, the date, the author, the David connection, are all subjects for conjecture. Wonderfully, what emerges is one of the most thought provoking and uplifting psalms.

There are several verses which have been used extensively in Christian worship: What is man that thou art mindful of him? Man is like a breath, and the final four verses are sublime Harvest Thanksgiving material.

This psalm is also reminiscent of both Psalm 84 and 18 which may have been source documents.

The use of the name 'David' in v. 10 is one of a small number of psalms naming David in the text as opposed to the title/superscription See also Psalm 89.3.

Psalm 145. In praise of God.

Book	V
Number of verses	21
Key verse	3

Type of psalm	Praise and another acrostic psalm
Possible original usage and setting	Recited or sung at either the Feast of Tabernacles or at the covenant renewal occasion
Including prayer or not	Both a hymn and a prayer (especially v. 10-13)
Individual or Communal	Communal
Date and author	Post-exilic, some say a very late psalm, although attributed by some to King David
Subsequent and Contemporary significance - Messianic indications	Contemporary Judaism uses Psalm 145 much in synagogue worship and it is also. much used in contemporary Christian praise, e.g. in the Church Hymnary CH4, as Hymn 100 and 101.

One of the dominant features of Psalm 145 is the ten-fold repetition of the Yahweh word for God, written as LORD in many contemporary versions.

The Loretto Sisters in their Psalms of Praise pamphlet (Conference Proceedings 2005) mention the wide occurrence of this psalm in both The Dead Sea Scrolls where the refrain, "Blessed be Yahweh and blessed be his name for ever and ever," is inserted after every verse, and also in the Te Deum, "Every day I will bless you and praise your name for ever and ever."

Praise is the defining mood of this psalm and as such it shows a strong universal sweep, *"The LORD is good to all, He has compassion on all He has made"* and *"The LORD is righteous in all his ways and loving towards all he has made"*. (Conference Proceedings 2005).

Psalm 146. Happy the man whose help is in God!

Book	V
Number of verses	10
Key verse	7

Type of psalm	Praise
Possible original usage and setting	Part of the daily morning synagogue worship
Including prayer or not	Not a prayer but a hymn
Individual or Communal	Communal although written in the first person
Date and author	Post-exilic, possibly dependant on earlier hymns
Subsequent and Contemporary significance - Messianic indications	These Hallel psalms from 146-150 are a microcosm of history, ending with continual praise, which is itself a messianic vision.

Psalm 146 may be the beginning of the final movement, the five psalm collection has been brought together and these five hymns form a grand finale. The fact that none of them have superscriptions reinforces their difference and perhaps gives a clue to their purpose.

The finality of this group of psalms is underlined in the severe warning in v. 3-4. This is indeed close in meaning to the parable taught by Jesus about the Rich Fool who wanted to build bigger barns (see Saint Luke's Gospel 12.13-21).

Verse. 7 is reminiscent of the prophet Isaiah 58 where the same lesson is spelt out (see Isaiah 58.6-9).

This wonderfully comprehensive short psalm draws together teaching from the Old and relates it to the New Testament. This emphasises the crucial role of the Psalter for students of both testaments.

Psalm 147. How good to sing praises to our God.

Book	V
Number of verses	20
Key verse	10

Type of psalm	Praise, part of the Great Hallel
Possible original usage and setting	Liturgical use possibly at the Feast of Tabernacles
Including prayer or not	Not so much a prayer as a loyal address to God
Individual or Communal	Communal
Date and author	Post-exilic, possibly sixth century BC, author unknown
Subsequent and Contemporary significance - Messianic indications	The theme of praise in this psalm is able to cross the centuries and move from Judaism to Christianity and still be applicable

Here is creation history and salvation history gathered together, and much more besides. This psalm may originally have been more than one psalm but the impact of the received text is undoubted. This hymn is everyone's hymn – young and old, women and men, poor and rich, those beginning a faith journey and for those whose faith journey is nearing the end. It is a hymn for all grateful people to sing and to say no matter what their condition or circumstances, but of course this can be said, and is said, of ever so many of the psalms.

There are points of connection with the Book of Isaiah (chapters 40-55) and other psalms e.g. 33 and 104.

Attention is particularly focussed on Jerusalem, and Jerusalem may also be understood as a messianic expectation as well as a present reality.

Psalm 148. Let creation praise its Creator.

Book	V
Number of verses	14
Key verse	13

Type of psalm	Praise (and part of the doxology to the whole Psalter)
Possible original usage and setting	Communal liturgical worship in Temple and presumably also in the synagogues
Including prayer or not	Not prayer but praise, but praise too is an offering to God
Individual or Communal	Communal
Date and author	Post-exilic, with author not known
Subsequent and Contemporary significance - Messianic indications	This psalm has served Jew and Christian well as a vehicle of praise

Here is a comprehensive programme for all creation to praise its creator. In ways, it is similar to and almost parallel with Job 38. Psalm 148 clearly has much in common with Psalms 146,147, 149 and 150 and they are one of three groups of Hallel psalms. The other two are the Egyptian Hallel, Psalms 113–118, and the great Hallel 120–136. Many of them include the admonition, "Praise the Lord" or synonyms for those words.

The repetition of the phrase emphasises the desire of the God of heaven to have the recognition of all his subjects: animal, vegetable and mineral.

Derek Kidner (1973) speaks of the 'choir of creation' which expresses the comprehensiveness of the instructions and he entitles Psalm 148 as 'The Choir of Creation' in his Tyndale commentary (pg. 487).

Psalm 149. A song of triumph with a threat of judgement.

Book	V
Number of verses	9
Key verse	1

Type of psalm	Praise
Possible original usage and setting	Possibly sung at the Feast of Tabernacles as the ritual of cultic drama.
Including prayer or not	Not prayer but praise
Individual or Communal	Communal
Date and author	Post-exilic, author unknown (an orphan psalm with no author suggested in the superscription)
Subsequent and Contemporary significance - Messianic indications	It has been tentatively suggested but not widely accepted that this psalm looks forward to the final judgement.

Praise is offered with song, dance and instruments. There is a charismatic atmosphere in this hymn. Verses 7 and 8 are frightening and yet lucid in their searing honesty. Is the psalm apocalyptic and does it look forward to that final judgement mentioned above?

Two motives may be identified. The first in v. 1-3 is a call to praise and to care for the needy. The second in v. 5-9 is a call to praise in the sound of the battle and to wreck vengeance and judgement on the enemies. Modern people will find v. 6 difficult. It is somehow not appropriate to praise God on the one hand and on the other call for God to wreak vengeance on the nations!

However, this is a victory song, and in every victory, there is a victor and a vanquished.

221

Psalm 150. Praise the Lord. Hallelujah!

Book	V
Number of verses	6
Key verse	6

Type of psalm	Praise
Possible original usage and setting	Whether this was written for Temple use or as a doxology to conclude the Psalter remains an open question, perhaps along with Psalm 149
Including prayer or not	Praise, not prayer
Individual or Communal	Communal
Date and author	Late post-exilic
Subsequent and Contemporary significance - Messianic indications	Echoes the praise of the centuries for Jews and Christians.

Probably the only place in the Bible with a ten-fold repetition of the imperative, "Praise the Lord". The range of musical instruments listed suggests universal praise, and indeed the praise of heaven itself. Indeed, it is a universal call to praise God. The hymn is the LOUD, LOUD, LOUD or the fortissimo of musical composition in the Bible.

Although this is not a prayer, the sentiment expressed in v. 6 is the fervent prayer of all believers for all humankind.

The psalm has given rise to many contemporary hymns and psalms. The Loretto nuns of Coleraine, in a publication on the Psalms of Praise, explain how the word for praise in Hebrew is 'hallel' and the abbreviated form of God's Name Yahweh is 'Yah', and that together these two, Hallel and Yah, make Hallelujah (Conference Proceeding's 2005).

.

APPENDIX TO CHAPTER EIGHT

Ps 1 Doing things God's way
Ps 2 God's chosen king
Ps 3 A strong man in trouble
Ps 4 God is my refuge, my joy and my safety
Ps 5 Help me in the morning, Lord
Ps 6 I'm sick Lord! A plea for healing and justice
Ps 7 Prayer of a virtuous man under persecution
Ps 8 Lord your world is amazing
Ps 9/10 God, the hope of the oppressed
Ps 11 The Lord is my refuge
Ps 12 We need God's help in a deceitful world
Ps 13 Sometimes it is very dark!
Ps 14 Are you really there Lord?
Ps 15 Who can stand before God?
Ps 16 The times have fallen for me in pleasant places
Ps 17 A plea for justice
Ps 18 The King's prayer,
Ps 19 God's creation and His Law
Ps 20 God save the King!
Ps 21 King by the grace of God
Ps 22 My God, my God, why have you forsaken me?
Ps 23 The Lord is my shepherd
Ps 24 He is the King of glory
Ps 25 Doing it God's way
Ps 26 Prayer of a blameless man!
Ps 27 God is my light and my salvation
Ps 28 Lord, hear my request!
Ps 29 The seven-fold voice of God
Ps 30 His anger is but for a moment
Ps 31 My times are in your hands
Ps 32 Forgiveness, repentance and instruction
Ps 33 My soul waits for the Lord
Ps 34 O taste and see that the Lord is good
Ps 35 I am your deliverance
Ps 36 Man sins and God rescues
Ps 37 Trust in the Lord and do good
Ps 38 Confessions of a sick and sinful man
Ps 39 Lord let me know my end

Ps 81 God calls Israel to obedience
Ps 82 God's judgment on false gods
Ps 83 Prayers during a crisis
Ps 84 How lovely is thy dwelling place
Ps 85 A Prayer for peace
Ps 86 The prayer of a needy man
Ps 87 Glorious things of thee are spoken
Ps 88 Face to face with death
Ps 89 God's covenant with David
Ps 90 From everlasting to everlasting you are God
Ps 91 Living with the Lord
Ps 92 Praise to the most high
Ps 93 God, you are forever
Ps 94 Judge over all the earth
Ps 95 Come let us sing to the Lord
Ps 96 O sing a new song to the Lord
Ps 97 The Lord is King!
Ps 98 The judge of all the world
Ps 99 Our God reigns!
Ps 100 All people that on earth do sing!
Ps 101 The perfect ruler
Ps 102 A prayer for restoration
Ps 103 Bless the Lord O my soul, and heal me
Ps 104 A hymn of creation
Ps 105 Israel's wonderful history
Ps 106 Repeated disobedience and restoration
Ps 107 For his steadfast love endures for ever
Ps 108 A doublet with Ps 57.7-11 and Ps 60.5-12
Ps 109 All about revenge!
PS 110 The Messiah and Melchizedek the priest
Ps 111 God's works endure for ever
Ps 112 The reward of the godly man
Ps 113 Praise the name of the Lord
Ps 114 Israel after the Exodus
Ps 115 Our God and their gods
Ps 116 What shall I render to the Lord?
Ps 117 Praise the Lord all nations
Ps 118 This is the day that the Lord has made
Ps 119 A eulogy on the Law of the Lord
Ps 120 Confessions of a peace worker!

Ps 121 I lift up my eyes to the hills
Ps 122 Prayer for the peace of Jerusalem
Ps 123 Eyes to the Lord!
Ps 124 Our help is in the name of the Lord
Ps 125 God's protection is around his faithful
Ps 126 Restore our fortunes O Lord
Ps 127 Unless the Lord builds the house
Ps 128 The blessings of a God-fearing man
Ps 129 Beware, Zion's enemies!
Ps 130 Are you listening Lord?
Ps 131 Child-like trust in God
Ps 132 God's covenant with David's dynasty
Ps 133 Families are precious!
Ps 134 A night hymn
Ps 135 A plethora of praise
Ps 136 For His steadfast love endures for ever
Ps 137 By the waters of Babylon
Ps 138 Confidence in God
Ps 139 Portrait of a man close to God
Ps 140 Deliver me O God from evil men
Ps 141 The evening sacrifice
Ps 142 Bring me out of prison
Ps 143 Teach me O Lord!
Ps 144 God in nature, in history and in providence
Ps 145 In praise of God
Ps 146 Happy is the man whose help is in God!
Ps 147 How good to sing praises to our God
Ps 148 Let creation praise its Creator
Ps 149 A song of triumph with a threat of judgment
Ps 150 Praise the Lord. Hallelujah!

BIBLIOGRAPHY

Anderson, A.A., (1972) *Psalms, New Century Bible Commentary*, London: Marshall, Morgan and Scott.

Anderson, B W (1983) *Out of the Depths*, Philadelphia: Westminster.

Barton J, (1984) *Reading the Old Testament*, London: Darton, Longman and Todd.

Bellinger, W.H. Jr, (2012) Psalms *A guide to studying the Psalms*, Baker Academic, USA.

Bonhoeffer D (1953) *Letters and papers from Prison* National Book Network London.

Bonhoeffer D (1969) *The cost of Discipleship* SCM London.

Church Hymnary CH4, (2007) Fourth Edition Church of Scotland, Edinburgh.

Gibran, Kahlil (1979) *The Prophet*, Heinemann, London.

Gordon, R N, (2000) *Transforming Psalms* Kachere Press, Malawi.

Gordon, R N, Hutchinson P (2003), *Psalms for Sadness, Sickness and Celebration*, Impact Publishers, Ballycastle, N. Ireland.

Bosch D (1991) *Transforming Mission*, Maryknoll Orbis.

IBVM The Loretto Sisters (2005) *Psalms of praise*, Coleraine, N. Ireland.

Jennens, C., Handel, G F (1741) *The Messiah, List of biblical texts Employed.*

Kidner D, (1973) *Psalms, Tyndale Old Testament Commentaries*, Leicester: Inter-Varsity Press.

Lewis, C. S. (1958) *Reflections on the Psalms*, London: Geoffrey Bles.

Longman T (1988) *How to Read the Psalms*, Leicester: Inter-Varsity Press.

Martini, C-M, (1990) *What am I that you care for me? Praying with the Psalms* St Pauls, First English edition.

Mays, J.L (1994) *Psalms, Interpretation Commentary Series*, Louiville:

John Knox.

McCullough, W.S., Taylor W.R. (1955), *Psalms, Interpreters' Bible Vol. 4,* New York: Abingdon.

McDowell H (1988) *On the Way to Bethlehem,* Oxford: Bible Reading Fellowship.

Miller, P D., (1986) *Interpreting the Psalms*, Philadelphia: Fortress.

Nouven H J.M. (1994) *The Return of the Prodigal Son*: Darton, Longman and Todd.

Peterson E, (1987) *Psalms, Prayers of the Heart.* Bletchley: Scripture Union.

Stolz F (1974) *Interpreting the Old Testament*, London: SCM.

Taylor H L, after Bunyan J (date unknown) *Little Pilgrim's Progress* Moody Institute.

Wink W (1980) *Transforming Bible Study,* London: SCM.

Bible Versions used with abbreviations

Authorised Version AV 1611

Revised Standard Version RSV 1952

New English Bible NEB 1961

New International Version NIV 1966

Jerusalem Bible JB 1968

Good News Bible BNB 1968

Peterson's The Message (Not so much a translation as a paraphrase) 2001

Phillips J B (1959) The New Testament in Modern English Geoffrey Bles. London

Useful Online Resources

Easy English Psalms Gordon Churchyard

Bible Gateway Psalms with notes

Agape Bible Study The Seven Annual Sacred Feasts of the Old Covenant

Introduction to the Psalms The Psalms and the Benedictines

Masterpost The Order of the Psalmody and the Benedictine Rule

INDEX

INDEX

Lightning Source UK Ltd.
Milton Keynes UK
UKHW02f1012290418
321814UK00008B/330/P